QUICK AND DELICIOUS VEGETARIAN MEALS

Judy Ridgway

A How To Book

ROBINSON

ROBINSON

First published in Great Britain in 2016 by Robinson

Text copyright © Judy Ridgway, 2016

1 3 5 7 9 8 6 4 2

Some of the recipes in this new book originally appeared in Judy Ridgway's successful *The Quick After-Work Vegetarian Cookbook*, published in 1994 and *The Quick After-Work Winter Vegetarian Cookbook*, published in 1996. These recipes have been adapted and brought up to date in the light of new nutritional information, and many new recipes added.

The moral right of the author has been asserted.

A CIP catalogue record for this book
is available from the British Library.

ISBN: 978-1-47213-660-2 (paperback)

Typeset by Basement Press, Glaisdale

Printed and bound in Great Britain by CPI Group (UK) Ltd, Croydon CR0 4YY

Papers used by Robinson are from well-managed forests and other responsible sources

MIX
Paper from
responsible sources
FSC® C104740

Robinson
is an imprint of
Little, Brown Book Group
Carmelite House
50 Victoria Embankment
London EC4Y 0DZ

An Hachette UK Company
www.hachette.co.uk

www.littlebrown.co.uk

How To Books are published by Robinson, an imprint of Little, Brown Book Group. We welcome proposals from authors who have first-hand experience of their subjects. Please set out the aims of your book, its target market and its suggested contents in an email to Nikki.Read@howtobooks.co.uk

CONTENTS

INTRODUCTION

Every year, I seem to have less and less time to prepare good nutritious meals but I do prefer home cooking to bought-in food. The solution has been to devise recipes which take the minimum of time to prepare and cook. Some people think that vegetarian food takes longer to prepare than other types of food but you will see that this is just not true. All the dishes in this book can be made in thirty minutes or so and many are ready to eat in a good deal less than that. This means that a two-course meal with fruit to finish can be made very quickly indeed.

When I started on this project I thought it would be quite a challenge: dishes such as casseroles, soups and stews are traditionally cooked for quite a long time, especially those that include dried beans; ideas for vegetarian barbecues are few and far between; and party food can be challenging. In the event it was a lot easier than I expected and I have come up with a complete range of dishes, from snacks and appetisers, starters, soups and salads to light suppers and all kinds of main courses. Almost half of these recipes are suitable for vegans.

My first discovery was that long slow cooking is not always necessary to tenderise hard vegetables. Root vegetables such as carrots, swede, parsnips, beetroot and celeriac will all cook quite quickly if they are first finely diced for use in soups and casseroles or coarsely grated for use in stuffings and burgers. They also stir-fry well if they are cut into matchsticks or wide shavings. To make the latter you can use a mandolin, a tool that consists of a blade mounted on a small frame; use it rather like a cheese slicer.

My second discovery was that you can give depth of flavour to a dish either by using a well-flavoured home-made stock or by fast boiling to concentrate, or reduce, the cooking liquor. With this in mind I try to save all the cooking liquor from vegetables, however they are cooked. I can then use this on its own or to make vegetable stock with other ingredients. I have given two recipes for vegetable stock on pages 10–11 and 12. Freeze the prepared stock in small plastic containers or ice-cube trays. You will then have stock to add to a dish without having to thaw a large quantity first.

Thinking ahead really does help in speedy cooking. Equally a well-planned store cupboard (see pages 6–7) can help to transform a simple meal based on a few vegetables, tofu, cheese, rice or pasta into an interesting culinary experience. A selection of sauces and pastes (such as green olive paste), canned pulses and tomatoes can make light work of food preparation. When shopping, keep your eyes open for new ideas. If you are a strict vegetarian you will want to use cheeses which do not contain animal-derived rennet (see list on pages 7–9).

Deciding on a menu for the evening only takes a minute or two and is inspired either by the contents of the store cupboard or vegetable rack, or by the fruit and vegetables on sale at market stalls or the supermarket on the way to and from work. Some of the most successful menus developed during the testing for this book are given on pages 13–14.

I do hope that this book will encourage everyone who has to produce fast food at home on a regular basis to experiment with different ingredients and only use the supermarket chilled food cabinet in an emergency!

CHAPTER 1
THE VEGETARIAN KITCHEN

A HEALTHY VEGETARIAN DIET

There is no reason why a diet free from meat and fish should not be as healthy and nutritious as any other. Indeed, vegetarians are more likely than most to eat a healthy diet that includes at least five items of fruit and vegetables a day.

Research confirms that a Mediterranean-style diet with olive oil at its heart is by far the best way to eat. Low-fat dietary advice is a thing of the past. The US Dietary Guidelines Advisory Committee has reversed forty years of advice to limit total fat and it is more than likely that this approach will be taken up elsewhere.

We now know that good fats, particularly monounsaturated fat such as that found in olive oil, are vital for good health. They are important in controlling levels of cholesterol in the blood and thereby helping to prevent coronary heart disease and other chronic conditions. In addition to olive oil, avocados, rapeseed oil, peanuts, hazelnuts, almonds, cashews, macadamias and their oils are all rich in monounsaturated fats.

Other nuts and seeds are rich in polyunsaturated fats, including omega-6 and omega-3 essential fatty acids that the body is unable to manufacture for itself. However, most of us don't get enough omega-3 and because of the widespread use of seed oils in the Western diet, omega-6 fatty acids tend to predominate, to the detriment of our health. It is important to watch the ratio between these two types of polyunsaturated fats: it should be around 4:1. Though fish and shellfish are the main sources of omega-3 there are vegetarian foods which contain reasonable amounts of omega-3, such as flaxseeds, chia seeds, walnuts and eggs.

Saturated fats are considered to be the least beneficial fats; in the vegetarian diet these are mainly only to be found in eggs and dairy foods. Although eggs contain cholesterol, the amount of saturated fat we eat overall has more effect on the amount of cholesterol in our blood than the cholesterol we get from eating eggs.

The traditional Mediterranean diet is not vegetarian, but only small amounts of meat and fish are included. The emphasis is on fresh, seasonal fruit and vegetables with unrefined wholegrain cereals, pulses such as beans, chickpeas and lentils, nuts and seeds. Dairy produce is usually in the form of cheese and yogurt, traditionally from the milk of sheep or goats grazing on varied vegetation rather than dairy-farmed cows. This could be important as the saturated fats in these traditional dairy products do not raise harmful cholesterol as much as other saturated fats.

The average vegetarian diet has plenty of protein from eggs and dairy products, dried and canned beans, peas, lentils, nuts and seeds. Vegans may find it more difficult to meet their protein needs. However, even foods that are normally thought of as carbohydrates, such as rice, bread, pasta and oats, contain significant amounts of protein. If some of these foods are eaten together they provide a more complete source of protein than when eaten separately. One of the best combinations is grains and pulses: examples include baked beans on toast, hummus with pitta bread, rice cooked with beans or peas, taco shells filled with refried beans or lentils.

A good vegetarian diet is naturally rich in vitamins and minerals. However, it is important to know that iron from vegetable sources (pulses and soya bean products such as tofu are particularly good sources) is more effectively absorbed into the body in the presence of vitamin C. Good combinations include wholemeal toast and orange juice at breakfast or a watercress and citrus fruit salad at lunchtime. Calcium is found in dairy products, but vegans can choose calcium-rich foods such as almonds, hazelnuts, sesame seeds, wholegrain bread, spring greens, kale, watercress and other green leafy vegetables. Lack of vitamin B12 can also be a problem for vegans, though it does occur in some vegetables – such as fresh, young bean sprouts. Yeast extract and soya milk enriched with vitamin B12 are useful sources.

The best way to ensure a balanced diet is to eat a variety of different kinds of foods. Snack on nuts and seeds or add them to breakfast cereals, soups and salads. Experiment with cereals and grains such as quinoa, bulgur and different types of rice, and soya bean products like tofu, miso and tempeh. Look for tahini (sesame seed paste) and dried seaweeds and combine them with everyday items such as potatoes, bread, cheese, fruit and vegetables.

Even if you regularly have to grab a quick snack or prepare a meal in half an hour, try to do something different every day rather than relying on a small number of tried and trusted dishes. The more you experiment the wider your range will become and the more nutritious your meals will be.

THE VEGETARIAN STORE CUPBOARD

Here's an idea of the range of foods I try always to keep in my store cupboard.

BASIC INGREDIENTS

These ingredients form the basis of many of my quick vegetarian recipes:

- Long pasta – spaghetti, tagliatelle, fettuccine
- Pasta shapes – bows (farfalle), fusilli, rigatoni, macaroni
- Chinese egg noodles and Japanese buckwheat noodles
- Rice – long-grain, basmati, risotto
- Quick-cook polenta
- Bulgur, couscous and quinoa
- Canned beans – red kidney, cannellini, borlotti, butter, black-eyed – and chickpeas
- Dried lentils
- Canned tomatoes and tomato purée
- Frozen peas, broad beans, green beans, sweetcorn and asparagus
- Flaked, ground and whole almonds, walnuts, pecans and pine nuts
- Extra virgin olive oil, groundnut oil

FLAVOURING INGREDIENTS

- A variety of dried herbs and spices
- Soy and Tabasco sauces
- Vinegars – sherry, balsamic, cider, white wine
- Mustard – made mustard (English or French) and mustard powder
- Sesame oil, toasted
- Dried wild mushrooms

- Sun-dried tomatoes – packed in oil, dry or paste
- Pistachio, hazel and Brazil nuts
- Peanut butter, cashew, walnut or almond butter
- Chestnuts – whole (canned or vacuum-packed) and unsweetened purée
- Canned water chestnuts
- Sesame seeds, pumpkin seeds and poppy seeds
- Green and black olives – whole and paste
- Pickled cucumbers and capers
- Dried fruits – raisins, apricots, prunes and mangoes
- Pesto
- Horseradish sauce
- Canned coconut milk
- Desiccated coconut
- Tahini and tamarind pastes
- Chinese sauces – black bean, plum, chilli bean, yellow bean

VEGETARIAN CHEESES

Rennet is an animal product that is used in cheesemaking to separate milk into solid curds and liquid whey. An increasing number of cheeses are now made with vegetarian coagulants of various kinds, sometimes called vegetarian rennet. There are vegetarian versions of most of the traditional English cheeses and some of the European classics. In addition, many of the newer English farmhouse cheeses are made without rennet.

Some traditional cheeses – including Parmesan, Pecorino and Roquefort – are not vegetarian because they contain rennet. They are made to traditional recipes and cannot be labelled with the traditional name if the original recipe is not followed. However, some companies produce vegetarian versions of these cheeses, and many UK supermarkets have their own brand of Parmesan-style hard cheese.

Feta and halloumi are traditional Greek cheeses that are often used in vegetarian recipes: however, some are made with animal rennet, so check before you buy. Similarly, mozzarella comes in both vegetarian and non-vegetarian versions.

The following cheeses are all made with vegetarian coagulants. Check out others on the internet and look for cheeses labelled 'rennet-free' or 'suitable for vegetarians'. But note that this information may be hidden in very small print.

FIRM AND SEMI-FIRM CHEESES
- Abbaye de Belloc (ewe's milk)
- Appleby's Double Gloucester and Cheshire
- Applewood Smoked Cheddar
- Cheddar – Davidstow, Pembrokeshire and many other Cheddars
- Cornish Yarg
- Cropwell Bishop White Stilton
- Devon Garland
- Muddlewell
- Sage Derby
- Spenwood (ewe's milk)
- Swaledale
- Ticklemore (goat's milk)

SOFT RIND CHEESES
- Bath
- Capricorn (goat's milk)
- Chabichou de Poitou (goat's milk)
- Cooleeney
- Cornish Brie

- Innes goat's cheeses
- Old Burford
- Saint Albray
- Sharpham
- Shepherd's Crook (ewe's milk)
- Soignon (goat's milk)
- Somerset Brie
- Stinking Bishop
- St. Killian
- Waterloo
- Wigmore (ewe's milk)

FRESH AND CREAM CHEESES
- Boursin
- Caboc
- Philadelphia cream cheese and many supermarket soft cheeses

BLUE CHEESES
- Bath Blue
- Beenleigh Blue (ewe's milk)
- Blacksticks Blue
- Cambozola
- Cashel Blue
- Cornish Blue
- Cropwell Bishop Stilton
- Devon Blue
- Dunsyre Blue
- Exmoor Blue
- Oxford Blue
- Shropshire Blue

VEGETABLE STOCKS

Fresh vegetable stock is available in supermarkets but it is very expensive for a small amount – not usually enough to make a soup. Here are two recipes for home-made stock which can be stored in the freezer and used from frozen. It is a good idea to freeze stock in ice-cube trays, so that if you just need a small amount for a sauce you can pop out a cube of stock.

These are the only recipes in the book that take longer than half an hour or so to prepare and cook. I usually get a stock going as I am preparing an evening meal and leave it to simmer while we eat. It can then be strained and the implements and saucepan can be washed up with the supper dishes.

SIMPLE VEGETABLE STOCK

Along with the basic onion, carrot and celery, you can use up any vegetables which are slightly past their best. But remember when adding swede or cabbage that they add a distinctive taste to the stock, which is fine if the stock is to be used with these ingredients but may not be so good with others.

You can, of course, make this stock with plain water, but for added flavour I save all the cooking liquid when I boil or steam vegetables, as well as the water from soaking sun-dried tomatoes or dried mushrooms. Yeast extract can boost the flavour of your stocks, but it needs to be used with great care as its distinctive flavour might be too strong for some dishes.

Makes about 750ml

2 tbsp extra virgin olive oil
1 large onion, coarsely chopped (but not peeled)
2 large carrots, scrubbed (but not peeled) and coarsely
  chopped
3 sticks of celery, coarsely chopped
3–4 large sprigs of parsley, with the stalks
1 bay leaf
a pinch of dried thyme
salt and freshly ground black pepper
1 litre water and/or leftover vegetable water
1 wine glass (125ml) dry white wine

1. Heat the oil in a large saucepan until it is very hot. Add the
    onion together with its skin and fry for 2–3 minutes or until
    well browned.
2. Add the carrots and celery and continue to fry over a high
    heat for a further 2 minutes. Reduce the heat and sauté
    gently for another 5 minutes. The mixture should not
    brown any further.
3. Add all the remaining ingredients and bring to the boil.
    Reduce the heat, cover with a lid and simmer for about
    1–1½ hours.
4. Strain and store.

CHINESE SOUP STOCK

This fragrant stock can be served on its own as a soup, with a garnish of small cubes of silken tofu and chopped spring onions, or it can be the base for other Asian-style soups.

Makes about 800ml

1 tbsp groundnut oil
1 onion, finely sliced (but not peeled)
1 carrot, scrubbed (but not peeled) and sliced into thin sticks
5cm piece of fresh root ginger, peeled and finely sliced
1 tbsp soy sauce
1 bay leaf
a large bunch of parsley
a few sprigs of thyme
1 star anise
1 litre water

1. Heat the oil in a wok or deep saucepan over a medium–high heat and fry the onion and carrot until lightly browned.
2. Add all the remaining ingredients and bring to the boil. Reduce the heat, cover with a lid and simmer for 45 minutes.
3. Strain and store.

VARIATIONS

Stir in bean or barley miso at the end to give a Japanese touch to the stock.

Instead of parsley and thyme, use lemongrass and fresh coriander, and stir in tamarind paste at the end to give a Thai flavour.

MENU SUGGESTIONS

Here are some of my favourite combinations for quick meals.
The desserts are up to you.

VEGETARIAN

Chilled beetroot and orange soup	53
Pasta bows with goat's cheese sauce	207

Chanterelles on toasted brioche	46
Soufflé omelette with stir-fried vegetables	113
New potatoes	

Liptauer cheese with sweet and sour cucumbers	23
Mixed root vegetable curry	130
Bulgur wheat with okra	229

Avocado and papaya cocktail	38
Carrot soup with curd cheese dumplings	72

Tomatoes stuffed with feta cheese	31
Spinach and chestnut filo pie	180
Shaken peas	236

Avocado salad with hot grapefruit sauce	41
Polenta rustica	230
Green salad	

Red cabbage and sour cream salad	76
Orange and mozzarella salad	77
Courgette and dill salad	83
Crusty bread	

Caldo verde	68
Fruit and nut salad	95

VEGAN

NOTES ON THE RECIPES

- Recipes serve 4 unless otherwise stated.
- Recipes suitable for vegans are marked (V).
- Extra virgin olive oil is used for most of the recipes in this book, but its distinctive flavour is too strong for some recipes, such as some oriental-style dishes. The best oil to use here is groundnut (peanut) oil, which does not have any flavour but which is rich in monounsaturated fatty acids and has a high smoke point.

  It is sometimes said that extra virgin olive oil is not suitable for high temperature cooking because the smoke point is too low. In fact, most good extra virgin olive oils have a smoke point at or above 190°C. The temperatures in a domestic kitchen rarely exceed this and so a good extra virgin olive oil can safely be used for all cooking methods. If in doubt about the quality of your extra virgin oil, use refined olive oil for deep-fat frying.

- The baked recipes have all been tested in a fan oven. You may need to increase the temperatures a little in other ovens.
- The ingredients are listed in the order in which they are used in the recipe. It's often a good idea to begin by preparing all ingredients that need weighing, chopping or grating so that you can whiz through the recipe. However, if time is short you may need to start one stage before preparing the next. Always read the recipe through before you begin.
- All spoon measures are level unless otherwise stated: 1 tsp = 5ml; 1 tbsp = 15ml.
- Eggs are medium unless otherwise stated.
- Individual vegetables or fruits are average-sized unless otherwise stated, for example, 1 potato = 1 medium (average-sized) potato.

- Can and packet sizes are approximate as they vary from brand to brand. For example, if a recipe calls for a 400g can of tomatoes and yours is 415g or 425g – that's fine.
- To skin tomatoes: cut a small cross in the base of each tomato, put them in a bowl and pour boiling water over them. Leave for about 30 seconds, then transfer to a bowl of very cold water for a few seconds. The skins should now peel off easily. To remove the seeds, slice the tomatoes in half and scoop out the seeds. If there is a hard, pithy centre, you may want to cut that out too. Tomato skins, seeds and trimmings can be added to vegetable stock, as it is strained before use.
- Toasting (roasting) brings out the flavours of most nuts and seeds. You can toast more than you need for one recipe and store the rest in an airtight container. Place a frying pan over a medium heat; when hot, add the nuts or seeds, stirring continuously to stop them burning, until they are lightly browned and aromatic. This can also be done under a preheated grill. Take care as most nuts and seeds burn easily.
- To hard-boil eggs: the eggs should be at room temperature before you begin. Using a slotted spoon, lower them into boiling water and cook for about 10 minutes. Drain and place in a bowl of very cold water until cool enough to handle, then peel off the shells.

CHAPTER 2
APPETISERS AND CANAPÉS

It can be difficult to find good recipes for vegetarian party canapés or appetisers to serve with drinks other than cheese straws, cheese on sticks and cheese-based dips. There are certainly even fewer vegan recipes. However, some years ago when I was running a small catering company I was often asked to provide interesting vegetarian food for parties. These are some of the ideas I developed at that time.

My inspiration comes from around the world, with dips from India, the Lebanon and Mexico and canapé toppings from Italy and Greece. To make a simple canapé base, cut a slender baguette into thin slices and toast lightly on both sides. Some of the recipes can be used either as canapé toppings or as fillings for pastry cases, small tomatoes, chicory spears and crisp Little Gem lettuce leaves.

The secret of successful party nibbles is attractive presentation. Think about mixing canapés with different toppings, and arranging them on a background of alfalfa sprouts or pea shoots. Presentation on wooden platters or mirrors can also be very effective.

Each recipe in this chapter will serve about twelve people as part of a spread of three or four party canapés. If you are making these for a buffet or as snacks you may need to make larger quantities.

LEBANESE CHEESE DIP
WITH BAKED PITTA BREAD

The recipe for this dip was inspired by my local Lebanese restaurant, where the chef regularly makes a dip with a cheese similar to ewe's milk feta. Look for feta or a feta-style brined ewe's milk cheese made without rennet.

4 pitta breads
2 tbsp extra virgin olive oil
3 tbsp sesame seeds

Lebanese cheese dip
300g feta cheese
1 tbsp water
juice of 1 lemon
3 tbsp extra virgin olive oil
1 red or mild onion, peeled and finely chopped
½ large cucumber, peeled and diced

Garnish
sprigs of flat-leaf parsley
slices of cucumber
black olives

1. Preheat the oven to 200°C/Gas 6.
2. Brush the pitta bread all over with olive oil. Cut lengthways into 1.5cm wide sticks. Place on a baking sheet and sprinkle with sesame seeds. Bake for 5–6 minutes until crisp and golden.
3. Meanwhile, make the dip. Mash the cheese with the water, using a fork. Add the lemon juice and then the oil and mix to combine. Finally mix in the onion and cucumber. The result should still be quite chunky.
4. Spoon the mixture into a bowl and garnish with parsley, cucumber slices and olives. Serve with the warm pitta bread.

BHURTA DIP (V)

This thick aubergine mixture from the Indian sub-continent makes an excellent hot dip to serve with pitta bread, as a filling for little tartlets or a topping for hot canapés.

2 tbsp groundnut oil
1 onion, peeled and finely chopped
2 large garlic cloves, peeled and crushed
¼ tsp cumin seeds
¼ tsp ground cinnamon
seeds from 2 cardamom pods
2 cloves
2 aubergines, peeled and very finely diced
2 large tomatoes, skinned and chopped
400g silken tofu
salt and freshly ground black pepper
175g frozen peas

1. Heat the oil in a saucepan over a medium heat, add the onion, garlic and spices and fry for 4–5 minutes. Add the aubergines, tomatoes, tofu, salt and pepper and bring to the boil, stirring all the time. Cover with a lid and cook over a medium heat for 20 minutes, stirring from time to time.
2. Meanwhile, cook the peas as directed on the pack. Drain and keep on one side.
3. Remove the aubergine mixture from the heat and mash with a potato masher. Stir in the peas, taste and correct the seasoning if necessary and serve hot.

OLIVE AND MASCARPONE DIP

Serve this rich and flavoursome dip with potato crisps, tortilla chips or, best of all, slices of toasted ciabatta bread. It makes a good appetiser with pre-dinner drinks, a party dip or an excellent late-night snack.

If you cannot find mascarpone cheese, you can substitute any kind of cream cheese but the result will not be quite so creamy.

12 stuffed green olives
12 large black Kalamata olives
250g mascarpone cheese
4 tbsp milk
1 tsp paprika
salt and freshly ground black pepper

1. Stone and chop all the olives very finely and stir into the cheese.
2. Add all the remaining ingredients and mix well together. Serve in a bowl with your chosen dippers arranged around it.

VARIATIONS

Use 2 tablespoons drained and rinsed capers in place of the black olives and add some freshly chopped basil.

Use 12 cocktail gherkins in place of the stuffed green olives and add some freshly chopped dill.

MINT AND CHICKPEA PURÉE WITH TORTILLA CHIPS (V)

I like to make quite a coarse, rustic purée, but if you prefer a smoother finish, simply blend for longer. Serve with plain tortilla chips to show off the fresh flavours of the dip rather than those which are finished with spices and artificial flavourings.

2 x 400g cans chickpeas, drained
juice of 1–2 large lemons
large bunch of mint (approx. 20 sprigs)
7–8 tbsp extra virgin olive oil
salt and freshly ground black pepper
1 pack (200g) plain tortilla chips

Garnish
sliced radishes and spring onions

1. In a food processor or using a hand-held blender, quickly blend the chickpeas with the juice of 1½ lemons.
2. Strip the leaves from the sprigs of mint, reserving one sprig for decoration, and chop finely. Stir into the chickpea purée with 7 tablespoons of the olive oil and salt and pepper to taste. Add more lemon juice or olive oil to taste. If the mixture is too thick but the flavour is good, add a little water to thin the mixture.
3. Spoon the purée into a large bowl and garnish with the reserved sprig of mint. Place the bowl in the centre of a large round or oval plate. Surround with tortilla chips and decorate with radishes and spring onions, which can also be dipped into the purée.

VARIATION

To make an even quicker dip, buy a large tub of ready-made hummus to use in place of the chickpeas and reduce the amount of olive oil to 1 tablespoon.

CURRIED CHESTNUT DIP WITH CRUDITÉS

This is an extremely quick recipe to make, but be sure to buy unsweetened chestnuts or you could end up with a very odd dip indeed!

225g canned or vacuum-packed unsweetened chestnuts
225g quark or low-fat soft cheese
1 heaped tsp curry powder
salt and freshly ground black pepper

Crudités
4 sticks of celery, cut into smaller sticks
10cm piece of cucumber, cut into sticks
1 large carrot, peeled and cut into sticks

1. Drain the chestnuts and reserve the juice. Purée the chestnuts in a food processor or using a hand-held blender, or rub through a sieve.
2. Put the purée in a bowl and gradually add the quark or soft cheese, beating well with a wooden spoon to ensure a really smooth consistency. Add about 2 tablespoons of the reserved chestnut juice, or water, to thin the mixture; stir in the curry powder and season to taste.
3. Spoon into a bowl and serve with the vegetable sticks arranged around the outside.

LIPTAUER CHEESE

This is a wonderfully rich concoction from Hungary. Friends in Budapest press it into a small pudding bowl, then turn it out and slice it. It is delicious eaten in the traditional way with sourdough bread and celery, but it can also be used in sandwiches with sweet and sour cucumbers and in salads with rocket and watercress.

175g soft cream cheese, such as Philadelphia
125g butter, well softened
1 heaped tsp paprika
½ tsp French mustard
1 tbsp capers, rinsed and chopped
1 tbsp chopped fresh chives
salt and freshly ground black pepper
sourdough bread and sticks of celery, to serve

1. In a large bowl, beat the cheese and butter together with a wooden spoon until they are very well mixed.
2. Beat in all the remaining ingredients and spoon into a small pudding bowl or large ramekin dish. Place in the fridge to chill for at least 1 hour. If you are in a hurry, pop it in the freezer for 10 minutes, but don't forget it.
3. Cut into wedges and serve on sliced sourdough bread, with sticks of celery.

FENNEL AND OLIVE TAPENADE (V)

Tapenade is a traditional Provençal dip made with olives and capers; in this twist on the recipe I've included another Mediterranean flavour – fennel. This versatile mixture can be served cold on canapés, decorated with a piece of feta cheese and a basil leaf, or warm on bruschetta, topped with slices of grilled peppers, tomatoes or aubergine.

300g fennel
100g large black Kalamata olives
½ tsp dried thyme
4–6 coriander seeds, crushed
a pinch of ground dried bay leaf
freshly ground black pepper
2 tbsp extra virgin olive oil

1. Trim the fennel, removing any coarse outer layers, and chop into small pieces. Place in a saucepan and add boiling water to cover. Bring back to the boil and cook for about 7–8 minutes until tender. Drain, keeping the cooking liquid for stock, and dry on kitchen paper.
2. While the fennel is cooking, stone the olives.
3. Purée the olives with the drained fennel in a food processor or using a hand-held blender, and stir in all the remaining ingredients. Serve warm on bruschetta, or place in the fridge to cool for about 15 minutes before serving on canapés.

VARIATION
To make a quicker version, buy herb-flavoured olives and blend with the cooked fennel.

EGG AND TARRAGON CANAPÉS

Tarragon is a perfect partner for eggs and this is a good topping for toasted slices of ciabatta or French bread. I sometimes use a griddle pan lightly brushed with oil to give attractive charred stripes to the toast. The mixture can also be served as a dip for crudités such as cauliflower florets or cucumber sticks – add a little more mayonnaise if using it in this way. Or it can be used to stuff mini pitta breads, together with a few lettuce leaves.

6 eggs
4 large sticks of celery, very finely chopped
8 spring onions, very finely chopped
leaves from 4 large sprigs of tarragon, chopped
4 tbsp capers, rinsed and coarsely chopped
125ml mayonnaise
salt and freshly ground black pepper

Garnish
small black olives

1. Cook the eggs in boiling water for about 10 minutes. Drain and cover with very cold water until cool enough to handle, then peel off the shells.
2. Chop the eggs (or mash if using as a dip) and place in a bowl. Add the celery, spring onions, tarragon, capers and mayonnaise and season to taste with a little salt and plenty of black pepper. Mix well together. Serve as a dip, or pile the mixture onto toasted French bread and garnish with small black olives.

PORCINI CROSTINI (V)

This is a very rich mixture and the canapés can be presented on a bed of strongly flavoured salad leaves such as rocket or watercress. You can also serve this as a first course for six people.

Save the liquid in which the porcini have been soaked and use to flavour soup or stock.

5g dried porcini mushrooms, soaked in boiling water for
   15 minutes
2 tbsp extra virgin olive oil
1 small to medium onion, peeled and finely chopped
1 garlic clove, peeled and crushed
175g open mushrooms, very finely chopped
125g open mushrooms, roughly chopped
2 tbsp dry white wine
1 large sprig of marjoram, chopped
4 sprigs of parsley, chopped
¼ tsp dried thyme
salt and freshly ground black pepper
1 tbsp ground almonds
6 slices of ciabatta bread, halved

Garnish
rocket or watercress

1. Finely chop the porcini and keep on one side.
2. Heat the olive oil in a saucepan over a medium heat and fry the onion and garlic until softened but not browned. Add the finely chopped mushrooms and fry for a further 2–3 minutes.
3. Add the roughly chopped mushrooms and the porcini with a little of their soaking liquid, the wine, herbs, salt and pepper and bring to the boil. Cook, uncovered, over a medium heat until nearly all the liquid has evaporated.

4. Stir in the almonds and continue cooking for another minute. The mixture should be quite thick.
5. Meanwhile, toast or fry the bread. Pile the mushroom mixture onto the toast or fried bread and serve with rocket or watercress.

GOAT'S CHEESE AND WATERCRESS PÂTÉ

There is no reason why vegetarians should not enjoy a good pâté. This one, made with a semi-soft goat's cheese such as a chèvre log, has a really tangy flavour. Go for a milder goat's cheese such as Chabichou if you prefer a lighter flavour. Serve with fingers of toast or baked pitta bread (see page 18).

200g semi-soft goat's cheese, chopped
6 tbsp quark or fromage frais
2 bunches of watercress, chopped
10 spring onions, finely chopped
freshly ground black pepper

1. Place all the ingredients in a bowl and mix well with a fork.
2. Spoon into a pâté dish and serve with toast or pitta bread.

VARIATION

For a vegan alternative, use 300g silken tofu and 100g ground almonds in place of the goat's cheese and quark.

AVOCADO AND SWEETCORN CANAPÉS (V)

This crunchy and appetising mixture can be served on rounds of toasted bread or on Mexican-style tortilla chips. It can also be piled into cooked vol-au-vent or pastry cases. It is fairly spicy but you can pep up or tone down the flavour by varying the amounts of chilli and coriander.

200g can sweetcorn, drained
2 small tomatoes, skinned and chopped
4 spring onions, finely chopped
½ small red fresh chilli, seeded and finely chopped
3 tbsp chopped fresh flat-leaf parsley
1 tbsp chopped fresh coriander
2 heaped tbsp puréed tofu
salt and freshly ground black pepper
1 ripe avocado

Garnish
sprigs of flat-leaf parsley

1. Mix all the ingredients except the avocado in a large bowl.
2. Just before serving, peel, stone and dice the avocado and add to the mixture.
3. Pile onto your chosen base and decorate with sprigs of flat-leaf parsley.

VARIATION
For a non-vegan version, you could replace the tofu with soured cream.

CHICORY SPEARS WITH MINTED CUCUMBER HUMMUS

For an informal beginning to the evening, serve your first course in the form of tasty appetisers with the drinks before sitting down to eat the main course.

300g ready-made hummus
175g natural yogurt
juice of 1 lemon
14cm piece of cucumber, finely diced
50g fresh mint, finely chopped
salt and freshly ground black pepper
4 heads of chicory, split into individual spears

1. Mix together the hummus, yogurt and lemon juice; the mixture should be thick. Add the cucumber and mint and season to taste.
2. Arrange the chicory spears on a serving plate and place a heaped teaspoonful of the cucumber hummus on each one.

MUSHROOM BITES

These filled mushrooms are perfect for a buffet, or hand them round with an aperitif or a glass of wine in lieu of a first course. Look for small mushrooms which are just opening at the gills. These are easier to stuff than closed cap mushrooms. They look particularly attractive served on a bed of alfalfa sprouts, pea shoots or green leaves such as baby spinach or lamb's lettuce.

325g full-fat soft cheese
3 tsp grated fresh root ginger
1½ tsp grated orange zest
salt and freshly ground black pepper
6 tbsp finely chopped chives or spring onions
750g button mushrooms
12–15 stuffed green olives, thickly sliced

1. Mash the cheese with a fork and beat in the ginger and orange zest, salt, pepper and about half the chives or spring onions.
2. Remove the stalks from the mushrooms and chop very finely. Stir into the cheese mixture.
3. Place a teaspoonful of the cheese mixture in each mushroom cap. Sprinkle with the remaining chives or spring onions and the sliced olives.
4. Insert a cocktail stick into each mushroom and arrange the stuffed mushrooms on a serving plate.

TOMATOES STUFFED WITH FETA CHEESE

These make delicious finger food for a buffet, or serve three or four halves as a first course with a rocket salad.

6–8 small to medium tomatoes
125g feta cheese, crumbled
125g cottage cheese
2 tbsp chopped fresh parsley
1 tsp dried thyme
salt and freshly ground black pepper
6–8 stuffed green olives, cut in half

1. Cut the tomatoes in half and use a teaspoon to scoop out the centres and seeds. Discard any hard pieces and chop the rest.
2. Using a fork, mix the feta and cottage cheeses with the herbs, salt and pepper and moisten with the chopped tomato.
3. Spoon the mixture into the tomato halves and decorate each one with half an olive.

VARIATIONS

Chop the olives into the mixture and decorate with sprigs of flat-leaf parsley.

Use finely chopped spring onion in place of the parsley and freshly chopped mint in place of the thyme. Decorate with pomegranate seeds.

TOFU CAKES WITH
SWEET AND SOUR SAUCE (V)

Cook these tasty little bites in batches and serve as soon as they are cooked. Alternatively, make larger cakes and shallow-fry as a first course or snack for four or six.

450g firm tofu
1 bunch of spring onions, very finely chopped
2 tbsp grated fresh root ginger
1 tsp grated orange zest
125g fresh breadcrumbs
2 tbsp soy sauce
freshly ground black pepper
4 tbsp rice flour, potato flour or cornflour
groundnut oil for deep-frying

Sweet and sour sauce
450ml pineapple juice
6 tbsp cider vinegar
6 tbsp sherry
3 tbsp soy sauce
6 tbsp sugar

1. To make the sauce, mix all the ingredients together in a saucepan and bring to the boil. Simmer for 6–8 minutes until it begins to thicken.
2. Meanwhile, mash the tofu with a fork, then mix in the spring onions, ginger, orange zest, breadcrumbs, soy sauce and pepper. Shape into small balls or cakes. Sprinkle the flour into a shallow dish and dust the tofu balls or cakes evenly with the flour.
3. Heat the oil in a deep-frying pan to 180°C/356°F; if you don't have a cooking thermometer, test by dipping a wooden spoon

into the oil – if bubbles immediately form around the spoon the oil is hot enough. Deep-fry the tofu cakes for 4 minutes. Drain on kitchen paper and serve hot with the sweet and sour sauce.

BLUE CHEESE TOASTIES

You can use any blue cheese to make these tasty cocktail bites but I particularly like Beenleigh Blue ewe's milk cheese or Oxford Blue.

450g blue cheese, crumbled
2 tsp mustard powder
2 eggs, beaten
freshly ground black pepper
2 tbsp port (optional)
8 slices of white bread

1. Mix together the cheese, mustard, eggs and pepper to form a smooth paste. Add the port, if using.
2. Preheat the grill to moderate. Toast the bread on both sides and spread with the cheese mixture. Place under the grill for about 4 minutes or until the cheese is bubbling.
3. Cut the bread into fingers and serve at once.

CHEESE DREAMS

Cheese Dreams was the name I gave to a range of fried cheese sandwiches when I was running a catering business in London. This easy-to-prepare finger food became the most popular item on the drinks party menu. I've suggested three of my favourite filling combinations, but there are many other possibilities. Use your favourite chutney or add a few herbs or spices.

450g Appleby's Double Gloucester or Cheshire cheese, grated
4 tbsp Branston pickle
12 slices of white bread
125g butter, softened

1. Mix the cheese and pickle together in a bowl.
2. Butter the bread on one side.
3. Place six slices of bread butter-side down on a sheet of baking paper. Spread with the cheese mixture and top with the remaining slices of bread, butter-side up.
4. Cut each sandwich into four quarters and each quarter into two triangles.
5. Heat a frying pan over a medium heat and fry the sandwich triangles until well browned on both sides. Serve hot.

VARIATIONS

Use 4 tablespoons curried fruit chutney instead of the pickle and add 2 tablespoons freshly chopped mint.

Use smoked Cheddar cheese and replace half the pickle with 2 tablespoons cranberry jelly.

CHAPTER 3
HOT AND COLD STARTERS

Whether you need an impressive first course for a dinner party or a dish that can be put together with a minimum of fuss to keep the family happy while the rest of the meal is cooking, you will find it in this chapter.

If you are very short of time, grilled vegetables are always a good standby. Slice peppers, aubergines, courgettes or fennel lengthways and cut chicory and radicchio into halves or quarters. Place on a baking sheet, toss with plenty of extra virgin olive oil and pop under a hot grill. They can be cooking while you make the main course. When they are charred and tender, drizzle with more extra virgin olive oil and serve sprinkled with chopped fresh herbs. It's a good idea to prepare more vegetables than you will need for one meal as they are excellent served cold later in the week.

Another really quick starter is baked feta cheese. Place a slab of feta on a piece of foil. Top with a small, very thinly sliced courgette. Sprinkle with dried herbs, season with salt and black pepper and drizzle with olive oil. Wrap into a parcel with the foil, sealing in the cheese, and bake in a hot oven (200°C/Gas 6) for about 5 minutes. Cut into four pieces and serve with more extra virgin olive oil and toasted pitta bread.

The recipes in this chapter are for four people. You could serve some of them as snacks or as finger food for parties. In the latter instance, double or treble the quantities depending on the number of guests.

HARD-BOILED EGGS WITH GREEN SAUCE

This green sauce is inspired by Italy's *salsa verde*, which is served with all kinds of cold foods, vegetables and salads: try it over warm new potatoes or mixed baby vegetables instead of eggs. Remember that you will still need one hard-boiled egg to make the sauce.

5 eggs
½ slice of day-old white bread, crusts removed
1 tbsp white wine or cider vinegar
2 tbsp chopped fresh parsley
2 tbsp chopped fresh basil
1 tsp chopped fresh mint
1 tsp capers, rinsed and chopped
3 tbsp extra virgin olive oil
water or lemon juice

Garnish
sprigs of fresh herbs

1. Cook the eggs in boiling water for 10 minutes. Drain and cover with very cold water. Peel one of the eggs and rub the yolk through a sieve. Discard the white or chop and use as a garnish with the fresh herbs.
2. Cut the bread into pieces and soak in the vinegar for 5 minutes. Mash with a fork and add the herbs, capers and sieved egg yolk. Mix well together.
3. Gradually stir in the oil, beating well with a fork until the mixture forms an emulsion and has a sauce-like consistency. If the sauce is too thick add a little water or lemon juice.
4. Peel the remaining eggs and cut in half. Pour the sauce over the top and serve sprinkled with fresh herbs.

LETTUCE PARCELS
WITH CHEESE AND NUTS

I first came across a cheese and walnut mixture in the hill town of Seggiano in southern Tuscany, where it was served with raw baby broad beans as a cheese course. In Italy, Pecorino cheese – made from ewes' milk – was used, but it is not vegetarian; look for a hard ewes' milk cheese such as Spenwood or mature Cheddar made with vegetarian rennet. This salad makes a very good starter stuffed into well-flavoured lettuce leaves such as Webbs, lollo rosso or oak leaf.

125g well-flavoured hard cheese, diced
50g walnut halves, coarsely chopped
4 tbsp chopped fresh parsley
4 tbsp extra virgin olive oil
1 tbsp wine vinegar
1 garlic clove, peeled and crushed
freshly ground black pepper
½ well-flavoured lettuce, leaves separated

Garnish
6–8 cherry tomatoes
sprigs of flat-leaf parsley
extra virgin olive oil

1. Place all the ingredients except the lettuce leaves in a bowl and mix well together.
2. Spoon the mixture onto the lettuce leaves and roll up into parcels. Garnish with cherry tomatoes and sprigs of parsley and drizzle with extra virgin olive oil.

AVOCADO AND PAPAYA COCKTAIL

I first enjoyed this at the Colony Club Hotel in Barbados.

1 ripe avocado
juice of ½ lemon
1 ripe papaya (pawpaw)
juice of ½ lime
¼ tsp cayenne pepper
3 tbsp coarsely chopped fresh coriander
3 tbsp natural yogurt

1. Peel, stone and dice the avocado and immediately mix with the lemon juice to prevent discoloration.
2. Peel the papaya and remove the seeds. Cut into pieces the same size as the diced avocado.
3. Mix both fruits with all the remaining ingredients and serve at once.

VARIATION
Instead of coriander, you could use finely chopped spring onions or parsley.

AVOCADO-STUFFED TOMATOES

Avocados are one of my favourite foods and I usually have one or two ripening in my fruit bowl. This mixture of avocado and thick yogurt is very versatile: I also use it to stuff sticks of celery or to fill small taco shells.

4 medium to large tomatoes
salt and freshly ground black pepper
1 large ripe avocado, cut in half and stoned
grated zest and juice of 1 lemon
2 spring onions, very finely chopped
1 tsp grated fresh root ginger
150g Greek-style yogurt

1. Cut the tomatoes in half. Scoop out the seeds and centres and discard. Season lightly and keep on one side.
2. Peel the avocado and immediately place it in a small bowl with the lemon juice to prevent discoloration. Rub the mixture through a sieve or process in a blender or food processor.
3. Stir in the lemon zest, spring onions and ginger and season to taste. Fold in the yogurt and use to fill the tomatoes.

MIXED LEAF SALAD
WITH TAPENADE CROUTONS

Tapenade is a salty Provençal dip made with olives and capers; it traditionally includes anchovies but vegetarian olive tapenade is widely available. Spread on croutons to add interest to any mix of salad leaves. Add some shavings of a Parmesan-style hard cheese and sun-dried tomatoes and you have a sophisticated light first course.

2 thick slices of ciabatta or olive bread
2 tbsp extra virgin olive oil
3 tbsp olive tapenade
mixed salad leaves
4 sun-dried tomatoes, soaked in boiling water for about
 15 minutes, then cut into strips
50g mature hard cheese, cut into thin shavings

Dressing
6 tbsp extra virgin olive oil
1 tbsp sherry vinegar
salt and freshly ground black pepper

1. Brush the bread on both sides with plenty of olive oil and toast under a hot grill or fry in a frying pan or griddle pan. Spread with the tapenade and cut each slice in half.

2. Arrange the salad leaves on four serving plates and top with the tapenade croutons.

3. Sprinkle with the sun-dried tomato strips and the cheese shavings.

4. Mix all the dressing ingredients together, spoon over the salads and serve at once.

AVOCADO SALAD
WITH HOT GRAPEFRUIT SAUCE

Grapefruit and avocado is a tried and tested combination in my kitchen but I wanted to try something a little more adventurous than simple grapefruit segments. This deliciously rich sauce complements the velvety texture of the avocados.

100g mixed salad leaves (curly endive, chicory and lettuce)
4 large ripe tomatoes, skinned and seeded
3 grapefruit
2 ripe avocados
1 box of cress
75g unsalted butter, cut into small pieces

1. Arrange the salad leaves on four serving plates. Finely chop the tomatoes and place in a sieve to drain.
2. Squeeze the grapefruit and strain the juice into a saucepan. Bring to the boil and boil rapidly until the mixture is reduced to about 4 tablespoons.
3. Halve, peel and stone the avocados and cut each one lengthways into a fan shape. Arrange on top of the salad leaves. Place mounds of tomato and cress around the avocados.
4. Whisk the butter, a piece at a time, into the reduced grapefruit juice until the mixture thickens. Do not let it boil. Pour this sauce over the top of the avocados and serve at once.

ARTICHOKES BAKED WITH GOAT'S CHEESE

This recipe is best made with canned artichoke bottoms rather than artichoke hearts. In my experience the latter tend to be stringy.

Any kind of fresh rindless goat's cheese can be used here but I particularly like the flavour of those with herb or pepper coatings: leave out the ground pepper if you use a pepper-coated cheese.

425g can artichoke bottoms, cut in half or quarters
175g fresh soft goat's cheese
6 tbsp natural yogurt
1 garlic clove, peeled and crushed
½ tsp dried thyme
freshly ground black pepper
50g fresh wholemeal breadcrumbs
2 tbsp extra virgin olive oil

1. Preheat the oven to 230°C/Gas 8.
2. Arrange the artichoke bottoms in an ovenproof dish.
3. Blend the goat's cheese, yogurt, garlic, thyme and pepper in a blender or food processor.
4. Spread the mixture over the artichokes and top with breadcrumbs. Drizzle with the olive oil and bake for 10–15 minutes until the breadcrumbs are browned. Serve hot.

STUFFED RED PEPPERS (V)

If I have time I like to make a double quantity of these delicately flavoured stuffed peppers. One batch is served hot as soon as it is cooked. The remaining peppers can be kept in the fridge for a day or so. They are very good served cold with an olive oil-based vinaigrette.

2 tbsp extra virgin olive oil
1 small onion, peeled and chopped
½ small green pepper, chopped
½ tsp paprika
50g cooked peas
75g long-grain rice
175ml vegetable stock
salt and freshly ground black pepper
4 small red peppers

1. Heat 1 tablespoon of the olive oil in a saucepan over a medium–low heat, add the onion and green pepper and fry gently until tender. Stir in the paprika, making sure it doesn't burn, then add the peas.
2. Stir in the rice and add the remaining tablespoon of olive oil and the stock. Bring to the boil, stir and reduce the heat; cook for 15 minutes until the rice is tender and all the liquid has been absorbed. Season to taste.
3. Meanwhile, preheat the grill. Roast the red peppers under the grill for 4–5 minutes, turning from time to time until they are well charred and beginning to soften.
4. Cut off the tops of the peppers and scoop out the seeds. Fill with the cooked rice mixture.
5. Return to the grill for about 5 minutes; serve hot.

GRATIN OF BROCCOLI AND CAULIFLOWER WITH TOASTED ALMONDS

This recipe is based on a technique I learnt many years ago at Roger Vergé's school of cookery at his restaurant, the Moulin de Mougins in Provence. It looks and tastes very grand but it really is quite quick and easy to make. Serve when you are entertaining or treat yourself to a stunning snack.

1 small cauliflower
1 small bunch of broccoli
150ml water
3 egg yolks
200ml double cream
salt and freshly ground black pepper
25g flaked almonds, toasted

1. Break the cauliflower into fairly small florets; cut the stalk from the broccoli and cut the head into florets. Place both vegetables in a saucepan with the water, bring to the boil and simmer for 10 minutes.
2. Drain the vegetables, retaining the cooking liquor, and arrange in four individual heatproof dishes. Preheat the grill.
3. Bring the vegetable cooking liquor to the boil, then simmer for 3–4 minutes.
4. Mix the egg yolks and cream with the salt and pepper and pour into the pan, stirring all the time with a wooden spoon. Cook over a low heat until the mixture thickens and starts to coat the back of the spoon. Do not let it boil.
5. Pour over the broccoli and cauliflower and place under the grill until the cream mixture starts to brown. Sprinkle with toasted almonds and serve at once.

GLAMORGAN SAUSAGES

These delicious little cheese sausages disappear very fast at parties. Larger sausages served on a bed of mixed salad leaves make an excellent first course. Caerphilly is the traditional cheese, but if you can't find vegetarian Caerphilly you might prefer to use Appleby's Cheshire cheese instead.

225g Caerphilly cheese, grated
175g fresh breadcrumbs
6 spring onions, finely chopped
4 tbsp chopped fresh parsley
½ tsp dried thyme
2 tsp English mustard
salt and freshly ground black pepper
4 small eggs, beaten
3–4 tbsp dry breadcrumbs
2 tbsp extra virgin olive oil

1. Mix the cheese, fresh breadcrumbs, spring onions, herbs, mustard, salt and pepper with about half the beaten egg to make a very thick paste. Shape the mixture into 12 small or 6–8 larger sausages.
2. Spread the dry breadcrumbs in a shallow dish. Dip each sausage in the remaining egg and then roll in the breadcrumbs to coat evenly.
3. Heat the oil in a frying pan over a medium–high heat and fry the sausages for about 2–3 minutes until well browned all over. Drain on kitchen paper and serve at once.

VARIATION

For an even more authentic Welsh flavour, use a small leek, or 3–4 baby leeks, in place of the spring onions.

CHANTERELLES ON TOASTED BRIOCHE

This is best made with fresh chanterelle mushrooms: dried ones simply do not give the same delicious flavour. It is important to use butter for it really does showcase the delicate flavour of the chanterelles. However, if you need to avoid butter the dish is quite good cooked with extra virgin olive oil and a splash of tarragon vinegar in place of the butter and lemon juice.

2 tbsp extra virgin olive oil
75g butter
4–6 shallots, peeled and finely chopped
2 garlic cloves, peeled and finely chopped
4 tbsp chopped fresh parsley
2 sprigs of tarragon, chopped
salt and freshly ground black pepper
125ml dry white wine
4 thick slices of brioche
250g chanterelle mushrooms, cleaned
juice of ½ lemon

1. Heat the olive oil and 25g of the butter in a frying pan over a medium heat and fry the shallots and garlic for 2 minutes. Add the herbs, salt and pepper and fry for a further 2 minutes.
2. Increase the heat, add the wine and cook for 5–8 minutes until all the liquid has evaporated.
3. Meanwhile, toast the brioche.
4. Melt the remaining butter in a saucepan over a medium–high heat, add the chanterelles and sauté for 1 minute. Add the shallot mixture, stir briefly to combine and serve on slices of toasted brioche. Sprinkle with fresh lemon juice just before serving.

AUBERGINE AND MOZZARELLA BRUSCHETTA

This elaborate bruschetta is quite grand enough to serve as a first course. Double the quantities for a good snack meal.

450g aubergines, trimmed
4 tbsp extra virgin olive oil
1 small ciabatta loaf, cut in half lengthways and then cut into
  two pieces
1 garlic clove, halved
2 tbsp tomato purée
12 fresh basil leaves
200g buffalo mozzarella, sliced
salt and freshly ground black pepper

1. Preheat the grill.
2. Cut the aubergines into 1cm thick slices and brush with a little of the olive oil. Grill on both sides until cooked through.
3. Toast the ciabatta on the crust side. Rub the cut surface of the ciabatta with the garlic clove and then brush with olive oil. Spread the surface thinly with tomato purée and return to the grill until toasted.
4. Cover with the aubergine slices and top with basil leaves, mozzarella, salt and pepper. Return to the grill until the cheese has melted. Drizzle with more olive oil just before serving.

ORIENTAL SWEETCORN FRITTERS

I usually serve these highly spiced fritters on a bed of salad leaves dressed with a little extra virgin olive oil mixed with light soy sauce. This recipe could also be served with stir-fried vegetables as a main course for two people.

250g cooked or canned sweetcorn kernels
8–10 spring onions, finely chopped
2 garlic cloves, crushed
2.5cm piece of fresh root ginger, peeled and grated
a few drops of Tabasco sauce
3 tbsp plain flour
½ tsp baking powder
salt and freshly ground black pepper
1 small egg, beaten
1 tbsp extra virgin olive oil

1. Mix the sweetcorn with the spring onions, garlic, ginger and Tabasco. Stir in the flour, baking powder, salt, pepper and beaten egg.
2. Heat the olive oil in a large frying pan over a medium–high heat. Drop tablespoonfuls of the mixture into the hot oil, to make eight fritters. Cook for 3–4 minutes on each side until the fritters are lightly browned. Serve at once.

SESAME-STUFFED MUSHROOMS (V)

A large flat mushroom with a rich tahini and herb filling makes an unusual first course; serve with wholemeal rolls.

4 large flat mushrooms
6 tbsp extra virgin olive oil
3 tbsp tahini (sesame seed paste)
1 garlic clove, peeled and crushed
2 tbsp chopped fresh parsley
1 tsp ready-made mint sauce
salt and freshly ground black pepper
1–2 tsp sesame seeds
rocket to serve

1. Preheat the grill. Cut the stalks out of the mushrooms and keep on one side. Brush the bases with some of the olive oil and place under a hot grill for about 5 minutes. Turn over, brush the gills with the remaining oil and grill for a further 5 minutes. Test with a fork to see if the mushrooms are fully cooked or if they need another minute or two.
2. Meanwhile, chop the reserved mushroom stalks very finely and mix with the tahini, garlic, parsley, mint sauce and seasonings. Add a little water to make the mixture spreadable.
3. When the mushrooms are cooked, spread with the tahini mixture and sprinkle with sesame seeds. Place under a hot grill and cook for about 5 minutes until well browned. Serve at once on a bed of rocket.

CHANTERELLES ON TOASTED BRIOCHE

The dish is particularly quick to make which makes it an ideal first course when you are entertaining. It is best made with fresh chanterelle mushrooms. Dried ones simply do not give the same wonderfully delicious flavour. It is important to use butter as it really does blend well with the delicate flavour of the chanterelles. However, if you need to avoid butter in your diet, the dish is quite good cooked with just extra virgin olive oil together with a splash of tarragon vinegar instead of lemon juice.

2 tbsp olive oil
75g butter
4–6 shallots, peeled and finely chopped
2 cloves garlic, peeled and crushed
4 tbsp freshly chopped parsley
2 sprigs fresh tarragon, chopped
a pinch salt
freshly ground black pepper
125ml white wine
250g chanterelle mushrooms
4 thick slices of brioche
juice of ½ lemon

1. Heat the oil with 25g of the butter and fry the shallots and garlic for 2 minutes. Add the herbs and seasoning and fry again for another 2 minutes.
2. Next add the wine and boil off completely. This takes about 5-8 minutes.
3. Pick over the chanterelles to remove any earth and wipe carefully.
4. Toast the brioche.
5. Melt the remaining butter in another pan and toss the chanterelles in this for 1 minute. Add the shallot mixture. Toss and serve on slices of toasted brioche.
6. Sprinkle with fresh lemon juice just before serving.

CHAPTER 4
SOUPS

Soups make a good start to a meal, and they need not mean hours of simmering. If harder vegetables are chopped into small pieces, and cooked with a really well-flavoured stock, excellent soups can be produced in a short time.

Some of the hot soups in this section such as Italian Bean Soup, Cauliflower Chowder, Spanish Lenten Soup and Tuscan Chickpea Soup with Pasta are thick and filling and can be served with a hunk of wholemeal bread as a main course.

Cold soups are appealing in the summer, but if the meal has to be ready in half an hour there is not much time to chill a cooked soup. The answer is to make soups which do not need to be cooked, using fruit and vegetables such as melon, cucumber and tomatoes with cream or yogurt.

When you have a little time to spare it is well worth making a double quantity of these soups as most of them freeze well and can be reheated from frozen.

All recipes are for four people.

TOMATO AND CUCUMBER SOUP WITH FRESH HERBS

Many different versions of this chilled soup have appeared on my table since I first tasted it in Sweden. There, dill is the chosen herb, but tarragon, basil or chives work just as well.

600ml tomato juice
1 large orange
125g natural yogurt
5cm piece of cucumber, grated
salt and freshly ground black pepper
4 tbsp freshly chopped herbs

1. Pour the tomato juice into a bowl and grate in a little of the orange zest.
2. Squeeze the orange and strain the juice into the bowl. Whisk in the yogurt and stir in the grated cucumber. Season to taste.
3. Place in the fridge to chill until required. Stir in your chosen herbs just before serving.

CHILLED BEETROOT AND ORANGE SOUP

Carrot and orange is a well-known combination, but orange makes an even better match for beetroot. The idea originated in Eastern Europe, where slightly sweet soups are very popular. Buy ready-cooked (vacuum-packed) beetroot, but do make sure that it has not been soaked in vinegar. It should also be well cooked: if it is underdone it will be difficult to obtain a smooth purée.

450g well-cooked beetroot, peeled and chopped
450ml natural yogurt
1 tsp ground coriander
salt and freshly ground black pepper
juice of 2 oranges
grated zest of 1 orange

Garnish
4 tbsp natural yogurt
4 sprigs of parsley

1. Put the beetroot in a blender or food processor with all the other ingredients, reserving a small amount of orange zest for the garnish, and process to a smooth purée.
2. Chill for 15–20 minutes.
3. Serve in bowls, garnished with a swirl of yogurt, a little grated orange zest and a sprig of parsley.

VARIATION
Vegans can use silken tofu in place of yogurt.

LETTUCE AND GREEN PEA SOUP
WITH MINT

If you dislike throwing away food, this soup provides a delicious way of using up the outside leaves of lettuces. Store leftover soup (or make double quantity) in the fridge for two to three days. The flavours will intensify to make an excellent chilled soup.

125g fresh mint
325g outer leaves from a Cos, Webbs or other well-flavoured
   lettuce
225g frozen green peas
400g (2 large) potatoes, peeled and finely diced
125ml dry white wine
450ml water
150ml soured cream
salt and freshly ground black pepper

1. Strip the mint leaves from the stalks. Chop half the leaves and keep on one side.
2. Place the lettuce leaves, peas, potatoes and the whole mint leaves in a saucepan with the wine and water. Bring to the boil, then reduce the heat, cover with a lid and simmer for 15 minutes.
3. Purée in a blender or food processor and add most of the soured cream, and salt and pepper to taste.
4. Pour the soup back into the pan, add the chopped mint and reheat. Serve in bowls, with a swirl of the remaining soured cream.

CELERIAC AND CARROT SOUP (V)

These two root vegetables combine to produce a sweet and velvety soup. There is no need for any extra herbs or spices – just use a good extra virgin olive oil and really fresh vegetables. When adding the stock, start with the smaller amount; if you prefer a thinner soup you can add a little more stock after you have puréed it.

3 tbsp extra virgin olive oil
1 small onion, peeled and chopped
350g celeriac, peeled and chopped
3 large carrots, peeled and chopped
salt and freshly ground black pepper
750–900ml vegetable stock

1. Heat the olive oil in a saucepan over a low heat and gently fry the onion until softened but not browned.
2. Add the celeriac and carrots and cook very gently for about 3–4 minutes, stirring all the time.
3. Add the salt, pepper and stock and bring to the boil. Cover with a lid, reduce the heat and simmer for 15–20 minutes until the vegetables are tender.
4. Purée in a blender or food processor, or rub through a sieve. Reheat and serve.

CORIANDER AND POTATO SOUP (V)

I am addicted to the spicy flavour of fresh green coriander and I have used it to give an interesting twist to this simple potato soup.

1 tbsp extra virgin olive oil
1 onion, peeled and sliced
2 garlic cloves, peeled and sliced
225g can chopped tomatoes
700g potatoes, peeled and diced
750ml vegetable stock or water
a pinch of dried oregano
1 whole green chilli
salt and freshly ground black pepper
4 tbsp coarsely chopped fresh coriander
juice of 1 lemon

1. Heat the olive oil in a saucepan over a medium heat and fry the onion and garlic for 4–5 minutes until lightly browned.
2. Add the tomatoes and their juice, potatoes, stock, oregano, chilli, salt, pepper and 1 tablespoon of the coriander. Bring to the boil. Cover with a lid, reduce the heat and simmer for 15–20 minutes until the potatoes are cooked.
3. Remove the chilli. Spoon into bowls and sprinkle with lemon juice and the remaining coriander.

BRIE AND ONION SOUP

This rich, creamy soup can be made with any Brie- or Camembert-style cheese, including Blue Brie. The idea for this soup comes from Germany, where many creameries make cheeses which are very similar to their French counterparts. Indeed, Blue Brie originated in Germany.

40g butter
1 onion, peeled and very finely chopped
25g plain flour
300ml vegetable stock
300ml milk
100g Brie-style cheese with rind removed, cut into small pieces
freshly ground black pepper

1. Heat the butter in a saucepan over a medium–low heat and fry the onion until softened but not browned.
2. Using a wooden spoon, stir in the flour until smooth, then stir in the stock and milk. Bring to the boil, stirring all the time.
3. Add the cheese to the soup, stirring until it has melted. Season to taste with black pepper and simmer for 5 minutes. Serve hot.

MUSHROOM SOUP

Home-made mushroom soup always seems to have so much more flavour than shop-bought, and it is not difficult to make. Use small button mushrooms for a delicately coloured soup or large field mushrooms for a darker, more robust soup.

1 tbsp butter
2 tsp extra virgin olive oil
1 small onion, peeled and sliced
2 leeks, trimmed and sliced
300g button mushrooms, wiped and sliced
300ml milk
450ml vegetable stock
½ tsp dried oregano
½ tsp celery salt (optional)
salt and freshly ground black pepper
3 tbsp single cream or natural yogurt

Garnish
1 tbsp chopped fresh parsley

1. Heat the butter and olive oil in a large saucepan over a medium–low heat and gently fry the onion and leeks for about 2–3 minutes until softened but not browned.
2. Add the mushrooms, reserving a few slices for garnish, the milk, stock, oregano and seasoning. Bring to the boil. Cover with a lid, reduce the heat and simmer for 20 minutes.
3. Purée in a blender or food processor or rub through a sieve. Return the soup to the pan.
4. Stir the cream or yogurt into the soup and bring to the boil, stirring all the time. Taste and correct the seasoning if necessary. Serve in bowls, garnished with the reserved slices of mushroom and a little chopped parsley.

SWEETCORN AND CAMEMBERT SOUP

You can use any kind of mild matured soft cheese in this quick-to-make thick soup. Serve with crusty French bread.

400g canned creamed sweetcorn
350ml milk
125g Camembert or similar cheese, rind removed, cut into
  small pieces
a good pinch of freshly grated nutmeg
salt and freshly ground black pepper

Garnish
chopped fresh parsley

1. Put the sweetcorn into a saucepan and gradually stir in the milk.
2. Add the cheese to the soup, then add the nutmeg, salt and pepper. Stir over a medium heat until all the cheese has melted and the soup is thoroughly heated.
3. Spoon into bowls and serve with a sprinkling of chopped parsley.

CRÈME DUBARRY WITH LEEKS

This variation on a traditional French cauliflower soup is particularly rich and creamy. Serve with hot French bread.

1 tbsp butter
1 tbsp extra virgin olive oil
2 leeks, trimmed and sliced
4 tbsp dry sherry
1 cauliflower, broken into large pieces
1 tsp French mustard
salt and freshly ground black pepper
700ml vegetable stock
150ml single cream
1 egg yolk

1. Heat the butter and olive oil in a large saucepan over a medium heat and fry the leeks for 2–3 minutes.
2. Pour in the sherry and bring to the boil. Add the cauliflower, mustard, salt, pepper and stock and bring back to the boil. Cover with a lid, reduce the heat and simmer for 20 minutes.
3. Purée in a blender or food processor or rub through a sieve. Return the soup to the pan.
4. Mix the cream and egg yolk together and pour into the soup. Heat through, stirring all the time; do not let the soup boil or the egg mixture will curdle. Serve just before it comes to the boil.

VARIATION

Use 125g diced blue cheese instead of the cream and egg yolk to give a piquant but still creamy taste.

CURRIED CELERIAC SOUP (V)

This simple soup makes a very quickly prepared and effective first course when you are entertaining. To serve eight for a dinner party, use double quantities of celeriac, curry powder and stock.

1 tbsp extra virgin olive oil
1 large onion, peeled and sliced
450g celeriac, peeled and sliced
1 tbsp curry powder
salt and freshly ground black pepper
800ml vegetable stock

Garnish
toasted pine nuts

1. Heat the olive oil in a saucepan over a medium heat and fry the onion for about 5–6 minutes until lightly browned. Add the celeriac and curry powder and fry for a further 2–3 minutes.
2. Add the salt, pepper and stock and bring to the boil. Cover with a lid, reduce the heat and simmer for 20 minutes until the celeriac is tender.
3. While the soup is cooking, toast the pine nuts.
4. Purée the soup in a blender or food processor, or rub through a sieve. Reheat and serve sprinkled with the toasted pine nuts.

VARIATION
Replace half the celeriac with parsnip.

FENNEL SOUP WITH GOAT'S CHEESE

Despite the distinctive flavours of the two main ingredients, this nourishing soup is surprisingly delicate. Look for bulbs of fennel which still have some greenery on them. You can reserve this and use to garnish the soup. If you have the time it is very good served with a sprinkling of fried breadcrumbs.

1 tbsp extra virgin olive oil
1 tbsp butter
2 onions, peeled and sliced
450g fennel, trimmed and cut into chunks
1 carrot, peeled and chopped
700ml vegetable stock
salt and freshly ground black pepper
175g semi-soft goat's cheese, rind removed, cut into
  small pieces

Garnish (optional)
2 tbsp extra virgin olive oil
6 tbsp fresh breadcrumbs
sprigs of fennel herb or green fronds from fennel bulbs

1. Heat the olive oil and butter in a saucepan over a medium–low heat and gently fry the onions for 2–3 minutes until softened but not browned. Add the fennel and carrot and stir with the onions for 1 minute. Add the stock, salt and pepper and bring to the boil. Cover with a lid and simmer for 20 minutes.
2. If you are making the garnish, heat the olive oil in a frying pan over a medium–high heat and fry the breadcrumbs until well browned. Keep on one side.

3. Purée the soup in a blender or food processor, or rub through a sieve. Stir the cheese into the hot purée, a little at a time. Reheat gently and serve garnished with fried breadcrumbs, if using, and sprigs of fennel or fennel fronds.

TUSCAN CHICKPEA SOUP WITH PASTA (V)

This is a thick, heart-warming soup from the Chianti Classico area of Tuscany. The locals pour it over hunks of country bread, and add plenty of extra virgin olive oil.

400g can chickpeas, drained
400g can chopped tomatoes
750ml vegetable stock
4 tbsp extra virgin olive oil, plus extra to serve
1 garlic clove, crushed
1 tbsp tomato purée
½ tsp dried rosemary
salt and freshly ground black pepper
50g small soup pasta

1. Purée the chickpeas and tomatoes and their juice in a blender or food processor. Stir in the stock.
2. Heat the olive oil in a saucepan over a low heat and gently fry the garlic for 1–2 minutes; do not let it brown.
3. Add the puréed chickpeas and tomatoes, the tomato purée, rosemary, salt and pepper. Bring to the boil, then reduce the heat and simmer for 5 minutes. Add the pasta and cook for another 10 minutes. Serve with plenty of extra virgin olive oil.

CHESTNUT AND ORANGE SOUP (V)

I used a canned chestnut purée made with roasted chestnuts, which gives a good colour and flavour. Of course, during the autumn you can make this soup with freshly roasted chestnuts, but it will take longer than 30 minutes to prepare!

2 tbsp extra virgin olive oil
1 small carrot, peeled and chopped
1 onion, peeled and chopped
100g mushrooms, chopped with their stalks
400g canned or vacuum-packed unsweetened chestnut purée
700ml vegetable stock
juice of 1 orange
salt and freshly ground black pepper

Garnish
grated zest of 1 orange
chopped fresh parsley

1. Heat the olive oil in a saucepan over a medium heat and fry the carrot, onion and mushrooms for about 5 minutes until very lightly browned.
2. Add all the remaining ingredients and bring to the boil. Cover with a lid, reduce the heat and simmer for 15 minutes.
3. Purée in a blender or food processor, or rub through a sieve. Reheat and serve garnished with the orange zest and parsley.

CAULIFLOWER CHOWDER

A large helping of this vegetable-packed soup makes a hearty main course. Serve with crusty wholemeal rolls.

1 tbsp butter
2 onions, peeled and sliced
1 large cauliflower, broken into florets
450g new potatoes, quartered or diced
100g frozen peas
100g frozen sweetcorn
900ml milk
1 bay leaf
a pinch of dried mixed herbs
salt and freshly ground black pepper
2 tbsp finely chopped fresh parsley, plus extra to garnish

1. Heat the butter in a saucepan over a medium–low heat and gently fry the onions until softened but not browned.
2. Add all the remaining ingredients and bring to the boil. Cover with a lid, reduce the heat to very low and simmer very gently for 15–20 minutes until all the vegetables are tender. Sprinkle with parsley and serve.

VARIATION
Try using broccoli in place of half the cauliflower.

QUICK WINTER BORSCHT (V)

A combination of root vegetables is the basis for this Russian-inspired soup. It has a wonderful deep red colour and a sweet and sour flavour. Non-vegans might like to add a dollop of soured cream just before serving.

2 tbsp extra virgin olive oil
1 onion, peeled and finely sliced
1 large carrot, peeled and grated
1 small white turnip, peeled and grated
1 stick of celery, trimmed and very finely sliced
900ml vegetable stock
225g cooked beetroot, grated
salt and freshly ground black pepper
2 tsp lemon juice
1 tsp tomato purée
soured cream (optional)

1. Heat the oil in a large saucepan over a medium heat and gently fry the onion, carrot, turnip and celery for 2–3 minutes until beginning to soften.
2. Pour in the stock and add the beetroot, salt and pepper. Bring to the boil. Cover with a lid, reduce the heat and simmer for 20–25 minutes.
3. Stir in the lemon juice and tomato purée. Ladle into bowls and serve at once. If liked, add a spoonful of soured cream on the top of each serving.

VARIATION

This is a rustic version of borscht. If you prefer a smooth soup you can purée the cooked vegetables in a blender or food processor.

SPANISH LENTEN SOUP (V)

The Lenten fast is strictly observed in many parts of Spain and chickpeas prepared in this way are extremely popular. I usually serve this soup as a first course as I find that too many chickpeas are a bit too much of a good thing! But if you would like to follow the Spanish custom and serve the soup as a main course, add extra onion, tomatoes, chickpeas and spinach.

2 tbsp extra virgin olive oil
1 garlic clove, peeled and crushed
1 small onion, peeled and chopped
a few strands of saffron
3 tomatoes, skinned, seeded and chopped
500ml vegetable stock
400g can chickpeas, drained
450g fresh spinach, shredded
salt and freshly ground black pepper

1. Heat the olive oil in a large saucepan over a medium heat and fry the garlic and onion until softened. Add the saffron and fry for a further minute. Add the tomatoes and cook for 2–3 minutes, stirring, until thick.
2. Stir in the stock and then add the chickpeas, spinach, salt and pepper. Cover with a lid and cook over a low heat for about 10 minutes. Serve hot.

CALDO VERDE (V)

This Portuguese soup is traditionally made with kale, but you can use any shredded green cabbage.

2 tbsp extra virgin olive oil
1 onion, peeled and sliced
350g potatoes, peeled and cubed
750ml vegetable stock
salt and freshly ground black pepper
225g kale or green cabbage, shredded

1. Heat the olive oil in a saucepan over a medium heat and fry the onion for 2–3 minutes. Add the potatoes, stock, salt and pepper and bring to the boil. Cover with a lid, reduce the heat and simmer for 15 minutes.
2. Purée in a blender or food processor, or rub through a sieve.
3. Add the shredded kale or cabbage and return the soup to the pan. Bring back to the boil, then simmer for a further 10 minutes. Serve hot.

VARIATION

Just before serving, add a small Boursin cheese and stir until melted into the soup. Serve as a main-course soup, followed by a salad.

ITALIAN BEAN SOUP

This delicious soup from Tuscany is served over a hunk of slightly stale bread to make a nutritious and filling main course. Finish off with a swirl of your favourite extra virgin olive oil.

2 tbsp extra virgin olive oil, plus extra to serve
1 onion, peeled and finely chopped
1 garlic clove, peeled and finely chopped
2 sticks of celery, finely sliced
1 carrot, peeled and finely diced
4 tomatoes, skinned and chopped
3–4 large sprigs of parsley
½ tsp dried oregano
½ small savoy cabbage (approx. 450g), finely shredded
1 litre vegetable stock
salt and freshly ground black pepper
175g cooked or canned haricot beans
4 large hunks of wholemeal bread

1. Heat the olive oil in a saucepan over a medium heat and gently fry the onion and garlic until lightly browned. Add the celery, carrot, tomatoes and herbs and fry for a further 4–5 minutes.
2. Add the cabbage, stock, salt and pepper and bring to the boil. Cook over a medium heat for about 15 minutes until the cabbage is just tender.
3. Stir in the beans and bring back to the boil.
4. Place the bread in four deep bowls and ladle the soup over the top. Serve with plenty of extra virgin olive oil.

SOUPE AU PISTOU

The flavour of this wonderfully aromatic soup from Provence depends on using plenty of basil in the pistou dressing. A 'bunch' in this part of the world means much more than a sprig or two – the more the better! Serve with plenty of crusty wholemeal bread.

Vegans can make a very good soup by substituting tofu for the cheese in the basil mixture.

1 tbsp extra virgin olive oil
1 onion, peeled and chopped
1 large leek, trimmed and sliced
1 large carrot, peeled and sliced
600ml water
3 tomatoes, skinned and cored
2 small or 1 large courgette, sliced
75g frozen sliced green beans
50g macaroni or thick pasta shapes
salt and freshly ground black pepper
150g cooked or canned cannellini beans

Pistou
3 garlic cloves, peeled and chopped
1 bunch of basil leaves
50g hard cheese, grated
4 tbsp extra virgin olive oil

1. Heat the olive oil in a saucepan over a medium–low heat and gently fry the onion and leek until the onion has softened. Add the carrot and stir to coat in the oil. Add the water and bring to the boil. Simmer for 10 minutes.

2. Add the tomatoes, courgette, green beans, pasta, salt and pepper and simmer for a further 10 minutes.

3. Add the cannellini beans and some more water if the soup is too thick. Cook for 5 minutes.

4. Meanwhile, make the pistou: grind the garlic with the basil in a mortar and pestle, or process in a blender. Blend in half the cheese and oil and then stir in the rest.

5. Ladle the soup into bowls and top each one with a dollop of pistou before serving.

CARROT SOUP
WITH CURD CHEESE DUMPLINGS

Dumpling-making seems to be a dying art in Western Europe, though dumplings are still very popular in Eastern Europe. These dumplings from Poland are easy to make and very light and fluffy. This dish may take just a little longer than half an hour to prepare and cook but it is worth the extra five minutes or so!

1 tbsp extra virgin olive oil
1 onion, peeled and finely chopped
500g carrots, peeled and finely diced
2 sticks of celery, diced
1 tbsp tomato purée
1 bay leaf
700ml well-flavoured vegetable stock
salt and freshly ground black pepper

Dumplings
1 egg, separated
1 tbsp softened butter
125g curd cheese or sieved cottage cheese
2–3 spring onions, finely chopped
2 tbsp plain flour
½ tsp ground cardamom seeds

1. Heat the olive oil in a saucepan over a medium–low heat and gently fry the onion until softened. Add the carrots and celery and fry gently for a further 3–4 minutes.

2. Add the tomato purée, bay leaf, stock, salt and pepper and bring to the boil. Cook over a medium heat for 15–20 minutes.

3. Meanwhile, make the dumplings. Put a large pan of water on to boil. Beat the egg yolk and softened butter with the cheese. Add the spring onions, flour and ground cardamom and season well.

4. Whisk the egg white until stiff. Stir a tablespoonful into the cheese mixture to loosen the mixture, then fold in the rest of the egg white.

5. Place 4 large tablespoonfuls of dumpling mixture into the boiling water and simmer very gently for 10 minutes, turning them over once.

6. Using a slotted spoon, transfer the dumplings to the soup and serve at once – remove the bay leaf before serving.

SWEET AND SOUR CABBAGE SOUP (V)

The inspiration for this hearty soup came from a visit to Bavaria, where it is served with black pumpernickel bread.

1 small green cabbage (approx. 350g), with the central stalk
removed
2 onions, peeled and sliced
1 very large potato, peeled and finely diced
1 large cooking apple, peeled and diced
600ml vegetable stock
300ml tomato juice
3–4 whole allspice berries or ¼ tsp ground allspice
salt and freshly ground black pepper
1 tbsp dark muscovado sugar
juice of 1 lemon

1. Shred the cabbage very finely indeed and place in a saucepan with all the remaining ingredients except the lemon juice.
2. Bring to the boil. Cover with a lid, reduce the heat and simmer for 20 minutes until all the vegetables are tender.
3. Stir in the lemon juice. Taste and correct the seasoning if necessary. Serve hot, with pumpernickel bread.

VARIATION
Use caraway seeds or juniper berries in place of the allspice.

CHAPTER 5
SALADS, LARGE AND SMALL

Many of the side salads I serve at home are made in a matter of moments using whatever I have in the salad box, together with dressings pepped up with flavoured vinegars, different kinds of mustard or fresh herbs. Do not forget the vegetable rack: celeriac, kohlrabi, leeks, cauliflower and broccoli can all be grated or chopped to use in winter salads.

Some of the salads in this chapter, such as Taco Salad, Chicory, Egg and Cheese Salad and Fruit and Nut Salad are substantial enough to be served as main courses. Others – including Fennel and Honey Slaw, Tabbouleh, and Courgette and Dill Salad – make excellent side salads. A medley of salads can make a meal in their own right: a very good combination would be Apple, Date and Chicory Salad, Watercress and Pistachio Salad and Red Cabbage and Sour Cream Salad. All recipes are for four people.

RED CABBAGE AND SOUR CREAM SALAD

This makes a colourful salad to serve in the winter months when red cabbage is in season. If red cabbage is not available, firm green cabbage can be used instead. Grate the cabbage on a coarse grater: this gives a much better texture than trying to shred it – I never seem to be able to get it fine enough, even with a sharp knife.

½ small red cabbage, coarsely grated
1 green apple, grated
3–4 tbsp soured cream
3 sticks of celery, chopped
6 small spring onions, finely chopped
50g walnut halves, chopped
salt and freshly ground black pepper

1. In a large bowl, mix the cabbage and apple with the soured cream and celery.
2. Add the spring onions and walnuts and stir into the cabbage mixture. Season to taste and serve at once.

ORANGE AND MOZZARELLA SALAD

Served with a hunk of Italian bread this makes a substantial snack. If possible, use buffalo milk mozzarella – it has more flavour and a better texture than the more usual cow's milk variety. Look for good-quality black olives: cheap ones are often made from green (unripe) olives which have been fast-cured with chemicals and dyed black with ferrous oxide compounds.

4 oranges
2 x 150g mozzarella cheeses, sliced

Dressing
6 tbsp extra virgin olive oil
1 tbsp vinegar
2 tbsp chopped fresh chervil
a pinch of dried mixed herbs
salt and freshly ground black pepper

Garnish
sprigs of chervil
black olives, stoned and cut in half or into quarters

1. To peel the oranges, place on a chopping board and use a small sharp knife to cut off the peel and white pith. Slice the oranges horizontally, picking out the pips.
2. Arrange the slices of orange and mozzarella on four serving plates.
3. Put all the dressing ingredients into a small bowl, mix with a fork and pour over the salads. Garnish with sprigs of chervil and olives and serve at once.

APPLE, DATE AND CHICORY SALAD (V)

This is a refreshing salad to serve as part of a salad medley or to accompany grilled or fried dishes.

2 dessert apples
juice of 1 lemon
1 small head of frisée (curly endive) or 3 heads of chicory
  (Belgian endive)
50g whole dates, stoned and chopped
1 stick of celery, very finely chopped
3 tbsp extra virgin olive oil
2 sprigs of mint
freshly ground black pepper

1. Core and quarter the apples and cut into thin slices. Toss in the lemon juice to prevent discoloration.
2. Tear the curly endive into small pieces or slice the chicory. Add all the remaining ingredients and toss well together. Serve at once.

ITALIAN BEAN SALAD (V)

This colourful and versatile salad can be served as a first course with some toasted ciabatta bread, as a side salad for a grilled vegetable dish or as a salad main course alongside two or three other salads. Choose Italian borlotti beans from southern Italy for this salad. The pale beans are streaked pink, which looks very attractive. If you cannot find them you could use white cannellini beans or red kidney beans.

1 large red pepper, cut into quarters and seeded
1 tbsp capers, rinsed and drained
20 black olives, stoned and chopped
1 tbsp chopped fresh parsley
400g can borlotti beans, drained

Dressing
4 tbsp extra virgin olive oil
1 tbsp wine or cider vinegar
1 tsp French mustard
salt and freshly ground black pepper

1. Preheat the grill. Place the pepper quarters skin-side up under a hot grill and cook until well charred. Remove from the heat and leave to cool slightly. Peel off the charred skin and dice the flesh.
2. Mix the peppers with all the other ingredients in a large bowl.
3. Put all the dressing ingredients into a small bowl, mix with a fork and pour over the bean salad. Serve at once.

WATERCRESS AND PISTACHIO SALAD (V)

This was inspired by the contents of my store cupboard one day. You can add baby artichoke hearts, onions in oil, olives, canned pimento strips or olive paste spread onto rounds of toast. If you have sun-dried tomatoes packed in oil, there's no need to soak them, just cut into strips.

3–4 pieces of sun-dried tomatoes
1 bunch of watercress or watercress tossed with lamb's lettuce
  or baby leaves
3 tbsp pistachio nuts, toasted
1 tbsp flaked almonds, toasted
sprigs of fresh herbs (parsley or chervil, basil, leaves and mint)

Dressing
4 tbsp extra virgin olive oil
1 tbsp well-flavoured wine vinegar
salt and freshly ground black pepper

1. Place the sun-dried tomatoes in a bowl and cover with boiling water. Leave to stand for 15 minutes, then cut into thin strips.
2. Strew your chosen leaves over four serving plates and sprinkle with the nuts and tomato strips. Dot with sprigs of herbs.
3. Put all the dressing ingredients into a small bowl, beat with a fork and spoon over the salad. Serve at once.

HUNGARIAN SALAD (V)

In Hungary I have had many salads that are marinated overnight in a light sweet and sour dressing which gives them a very attractive flavour. However, if you haven't time to marinate you can achieve a similar flavour by mixing sweet and sour preserved cucumbers into a fresh vegetable salad.

1 sweet and sour cucumber or large gherkin, very thinly sliced
1 small fresh pickling cucumber, very thinly sliced
1 small red pepper, seeded and very thinly sliced
1 carrot, peeled and coarsely grated
2 tbsp lemon juice
a pinch each of paprika and caraway seeds

1. Place the cucumbers in a bowl together with a little of the liquid from the sweet and sour cucumber jar.
2. Add the red pepper and carrot and toss with the cucumbers.
3. Add the lemon juice, paprika and caraway seeds and stir gently to combine.

ORANGE AND GOAT'S CHEESE SALAD

This salad can be made with almost any kind of goat's cheese log – for example one coated in herbs or paprika – but not too strong or it will overpower the orange and walnuts.

2 oranges
leaves from 1 small lettuce
½ bunch of watercress, trimmed
2 x 175g log-shaped goat's cheese, sliced
12 walnut halves, coarsely chopped

Dressing
6 tbsp extra virgin olive oil
1 tbsp sherry vinegar
salt and freshly ground black pepper

1. Grate the zest from the oranges and set aside to use for the dressing. Put the oranges on a sturdy plate and use a small sharp knife to cut off the peel and white pith. Segment the oranges, working the knife between the flesh and the membrane. Reserve the juice that collects on the plate and set aside for the dressing.

2. Tear the lettuce leaves into smaller pieces and mix with the watercress. Place the mixture on four serving plates.

3. Arrange four or five slices of goat's cheese on the leaves in the centre of each plate. Place the orange segments around the cheese and sprinkle with walnuts.

4. Put the olive oil, vinegar, salt and pepper into a small bowl and add 1 tablespoon of the reserved orange juice, plus a little of the grated zest. Beat well with a fork, pour over the salad and serve at once.

COURGETTE AND DILL SALAD (V)

Moulded salads like this look very attractive on the plate, either as a first course or as a centrepiece for a cold meal. Alternatively serve with baked potatoes as a simple supper.

225g courgettes
2 small carrots, peeled
¼ small green pepper, seeded
50g tofu or soft cheese
2 tbsp chopped fresh dill
salt and freshly ground black pepper
mixed baby salad leaves

1. Coarsely grate the courgettes, and then finely grate the carrots. Finely slice the green pepper and mix with the other vegetables in a bowl.
2. Add the tofu or soft cheese, the dill, salt and pepper, and mix well.
3. Spoon the mixture into four small ramekin dishes, pressing down well.
4. Turn out onto a bed of salad leaves and serve at once.

WARM CAULIFLOWER AND CAPER SALAD (V)

This is a simple but effective salad which makes a good first course for a dinner party.

4 baby cauliflowers or half a large one
1 thick slice of white or wholemeal bread, crust removed
4 tbsp herb- or garlic-flavoured olive oil
mixed salad leaves
½ red or mild onion, peeled and cut into fine rings
2 tbsp finely chopped fresh parsley
1 tbsp capers, drained and rinsed
2 tsp cider or wine vinegar
salt and freshly ground black pepper

1. Preheat the oven to 200°C/Gas 6.
2. Cut the baby cauliflowers in half or the larger one into four pieces. Steam for 5–6 minutes to soften slightly.
3. Drizzle the bread with about 1 tablespoon of the flavoured oil and place on a baking sheet. Bake for 5 minutes until crisp and golden. Cut into small cubes.
4. To assemble the salad, arrange the salad leaves on four plates. Cut the steamed cauliflower into smaller chunks and place on the leaves. Scatter the bread cubes, onion rings, parsley and capers over the top.
5. In a small bowl, beat the remaining flavoured oil with the vinegar, salt and pepper and spoon over each salad. Serve at once.

VARIATION
Rub a hard-boiled egg through a sieve and sprinkle over the salad.

LEMON, BEAN AND ALMOND SALAD (V)

This mixed bean salad makes a colourful first course or it can be served together with other salads as a main course.

175g flat green beans (runner or helda), trimmed and strung
50g green (French) beans, trimmed
salt and freshly ground black pepper
75g canned red kidney beans
25g flaked almonds, toasted
3 tbsp extra virgin olive oil
juice of 1 lemon
a little grated lemon zest

1. Cut both types of green beans into 2.5cm lengths. Add to a saucepan of salted boiling water and cook for 5 minutes. Drain and cool under cold running water. Drain again and dry on kitchen paper.
2. Mix the cooked green beans with the kidney beans and flaked almonds and spoon into a bowl.
3. In a small bowl, mix the olive oil, lemon juice and zest, salt and pepper with a fork and pour over the salad. Toss and serve.

VARIATION
Use a small orange in place of the lemon and add a dash of cider vinegar to the dressing.

MIXED WINTER VEGETABLE SALAD (V)

This salad combines cabbage with other seasonal vegetables. You can substitute whatever you happen to have in the vegetable rack for one or other of the vegetables given here.

1 large carrot, peeled and coarsely grated
1 parsnip, peeled and coarsely grated
juice of 1 lemon
1 cabbage (savoy, green, red or white), very finely shredded
1 small onion, peeled and cut into fine rings
2 cooked beetroot, diced
3 tbsp extra virgin olive oil
salt and freshly ground black pepper

1. Put the carrot and parsnip in a large bowl, add the lemon juice and toss well to prevent discoloration.
2. Add the remaining vegetables, the oil, salt and pepper and toss well. This salad can be kept in the fridge for up to half an hour before serving.

VARIATION

For a more exotic flavour, mix 1 tablespoon light soy sauce with the oil.

KOHLRABI AND RED PEPPER SALAD (V)

Raw kohlrabi has a lovely crunchy texture which works well in this winter salad with an oriental slant. Serve on its own as a first course, or with Fennel and Honey Slaw (see page 88) and a green salad.

1 large kohlrabi, peeled
1 large red pepper, seeded and shredded
2 sticks of celery, trimmed and finely sliced
3 tbsp roasted peanuts
1 tbsp chopped fresh mint

Warm dressing
4 tbsp groundnut oil
2 tbsp light soy sauce
2 tsp cider vinegar
salt and freshly ground black pepper

1. Finely slice the kohlrabi and cut into thin sticks. Place in a bowl and mix with the pepper, celery, peanuts and mint.
2. Put all the dressing ingredients in a small saucepan and heat gently. Do not let the mixture get too hot. Pour over the salad and serve at once.

VARIATIONS

Use fresh coriander instead of mint and add a pinch of five-spice powder, but take care not to use too much or it will dominate the other flavours.

Use mooli (daikon) or Jerusalem artichoke instead of kohlrabi.

FENNEL AND HONEY SLAW

This well-flavoured slaw makes a change from the usual cabbage mixture sold in the supermarket. The idea comes from a Canadian friend who really fell for the taste of early spring fennel on a visit to Italy. English fennel tends to be stronger in flavour and harder in texture than Italian fennel, so you may want to blanch it first.

175g white cabbage, very finely shredded
1 large bulb of fennel, trimmed, cut in half and very finely
  shredded
2 sticks of celery, cut into thin 4cm-long sticks
150ml soured cream or Greek-style yogurt
1 tbsp clear honey
1 tbsp cider vinegar
½ tsp French mustard
¼ tsp cayenne pepper
a pinch of salt

1. Mix the cabbage, fennel and celery in a bowl and cover with boiling water. Leave to stand for 1 minute, then drain. Then plunge the vegetables into very cold water. Drain again and dry on kitchen paper. Return to the dry bowl.
2. Put all the remaining ingredients into a small bowl and mix with a fork. Pour the dressing over the vegetables and toss well so that everything is coated with the dressing. Serve at once.

FENNEL, CHICORY AND APPLE SALAD (V)

All these ingredients are fairly easy to find during the winter months and together they make an unusual salad. Serve as a side salad or as a crunchy first course before a casserole or curry.

1 bulb of fennel, trimmed
juice of ½ lemon
2 green apples, cored and diced
2 heads of chicory, sliced
2 tbsp extra virgin olive oil
salt and freshly ground black pepper

1. Shred the fennel as finely as you can and mix with the lemon juice. Place in the fridge for 15 minutes or until required.
2. Add the diced apple and chicory and mix well. Pour on the olive oil and season to taste. Toss with a fork and serve.

VARIATIONS
For a creamier salad use mayonnaise in place of olive oil.
Add chopped smoked tofu, hard-boiled eggs or cubes of cheese to make a more substantial dish.

TABBOULEH (V)

There are numerous versions of this popular Middle Eastern salad, but they all rely on freshly chopped flat-leaf parsley. This is a fairly elaborate and colourful version which I like to serve alongside other salads. It can also be used to stuff chicory spears, cherry tomato halves and celery sticks.

75g bulgur wheat
1 large bunch of flat-leaf parsley, finely chopped
4 spring onions, finely chopped
2 tomatoes, skinned, seeded and chopped
7cm piece of cucumber, diced
½ green pepper, seeded and finely chopped
3 tbsp finely chopped mint
1 tbsp paprika
juice of 1 lemon
3 tbsp extra virgin olive oil
salt and freshly ground black pepper

1. Put the bulgur in a bowl and cover with cold water. Leave to stand for 20 minutes.
2. Drain well and then squeeze out all the water with your hands. Dry on kitchen paper.
3. While the bulgur is soaking, prepare all the remaining ingredients and mix together in a bowl.
4. Stir in the well-drained bulgur. Taste to check the seasoning and add a little more lemon juice if you like a sharper flavour.

VARIATIONS

Use 100g ready-to-eat dried apricots, finely chopped, and 25g toasted pine nuts in place of the tomatoes and cucumber.

For a really simple tabbouleh, use only the bulgur, parsley, spring onions, mint, lemon juice and olive oil.

TACO SALAD (V)

This crunchy salad has a definite Mexican theme and is very versatile. Excellent as a side salad or first course – or add beans, olives and cheese for a good main-course salad.

1 small avocado
1 tbsp lemon juice
mixed salad leaves
½ bunch or bag of watercress
5–6 sprigs of coriander
3–4 sun-dried peppers or 5–6 sun-dried tomatoes, soaked in
  boiling water for about 15 minutes, then cut into thin strips
1 green chilli, seeded and cut into very thin rings (optional)
75g plain tortilla chips, coarsely crushed

Dressing
3 tbsp extra virgin olive oil
2 tsp wine or cider vinegar
salt and freshly ground black pepper

1. Peel, stone and cube the avocado and immediately mix with the lemon juice to prevent discoloration.
2. Mix the salad leaves with the watercress and coriander in a large bowl.
3. Add the avocado, sun-dried vegetable strips, sliced chilli, if using, and crushed tortilla chips.
4. Put all the dressing ingredients into a small bowl, mix with a fork and pour over the salad. Toss well together and serve at once (if you leave this salad to stand the tortilla chips will go soggy).

VARIATION
Add 4 tablespoons cooked or canned red kidney beans, 8–12 stoned black olives and 100g cubed Cheddar cheese.

BEETROOT AND ORANGE SALAD
WITH HORSERADISH (V)

Fresh horseradish needs a very sharp knife to peel it; it also needs very careful handling because it contains compounds that irritate your eyes and the membranes in your nose, so wear thin rubber or plastic gloves and keep your fingers away from your eyes. I find that it is much easier to buy a jar of ready-grated horseradish which can be stored in the fridge for quite a long time. Remember that both the freshly grated root and the ready-grated horseradish are much stronger than creamed horseradish, so if you use the latter you will need to add more than the quantity given in the recipe.

225g raw beetroot, peeled
3 spring onions, finely chopped
2cm piece of cucumber, finely chopped
2 tbsp extra virgin olive oil
1 orange
1 tsp grated horseradish
salt and freshly ground black pepper
1 green dessert apple
1 tbsp lemon juice

1. Grate the beetroot into a bowl using a fine grater, or in a food processor. Stir in the spring onions, cucumber and olive oil.
2. Grate a little of the orange zest into the beetroot mixture and stir in the grated horseradish and seasoning.
3. Put the orange on a sturdy plate or chopping board and use a small sharp knife to cut off the peel and white pith. Segment the orange, working the knife between the flesh and the membrane. Cut each segment into four or five small pieces.

4. Core and dice the apple and immediately mix with the lemon juice to prevent discoloration.
5. Add the orange pieces and diced apple to the beetroot mixture. Stir and serve.

CHICORY, EGG AND CHEESE SALAD

This substantial salad makes an excellent main course. Serve with wholemeal rolls.

3 eggs
3 heads of chicory
100g firm cheese, such as Cheddar
3 tbsp mayonnaise
salt and freshly ground black pepper
rocket or mixed baby salad leaves, to serve

1. Cook the eggs in boiling water for 12–15 minutes. Drain and cover with very cold water until cool enough to handle, then peel off the shells.
2. While the eggs are cooking, slice the chicory into rounds and cube the cheese. Mix with the mayonnaise.
3. Chop the eggs and add to the chicory mixture. Season to taste and serve on a bed of rocket or salad leaves.

WARM MANGO, RICE AND QUINOA SALAD WITH SEAWEED (V)

If you haven't used arame (a type of dried seaweed) before, this is a good dish with which to start. The dark strands of seaweed look attractive in contrast to the bright mango, and the flavours blend beautifully. The salad is good warm but it can also be served cold.

50g long-grain rice
25g quinoa
175ml boiling water
1 tbsp extra virgin olive oil
3 shallots or 1 small red onion, peeled and finely sliced
1 garlic clove, peeled and crushed
40g sun-dried peppers, soaked in boiling water for about
    15 minutes
25g arame, soaked in cold water for about 15 minutes
1 large mango, peeled and sliced
2 tbsp lemon juice
salt and freshly ground black pepper

1. Put the rice and quinoa in a saucepan, add the boiling water and cook over a medium heat for about 15–20 minutes until both are tender (they will have absorbed all the water). Put the cooked rice and quinoa into a bowl.
2. While the rice is cooking, heat the olive oil in a small saucepan over a medium heat, add the shallots or onion and garlic and cook for a minute or two until softened. Add to the bowl with the rice and quinoa.
3. Drain the peppers and arame and dry on kitchen paper. Add to the rice mixture with the mango, lemon juice, salt and pepper, and toss well together. Serve warm or cold.

FRUIT AND NUT SALAD (V)

This is a really chunky salad which can be served on its own or as part of a medley of salads. If you are planning to make it the main part of the meal, increase the quantities by about a third.

leaves from 1 small tender-leaved lettuce
2 green apples
2 bananas
juice of ½ lemon
2 tbsp raisins
½ head of celery, trimmed and chopped
1 small red pepper, seeded and chopped
50g cashew nuts
50g pistachio nuts
25g sunflower seeds

Dressing
3 tbsp extra virgin olive oil
a little cider vinegar
salt and freshly ground black pepper

Garnish
a few whole chives

1. Arrange the lettuce leaves on four serving plates.
2. Core and dice the apples; peel and slice the bananas; place both in a bowl and toss in the lemon juice immediately they are cut. Stir in the raisins, celery and red pepper.
3. Put the nuts and sunflower seeds in a dry frying pan over a medium heat, stirring continuously to stop them burning. When they are lightly browned, add to the apple mixture and spoon the mixture over the lettuce leaves.
4. Put all the dressing ingredients into a small bowl and mix with a fork. Pour over the salads and garnish with long pieces of chive.

ITALIAN CHEESE AND WALNUT SALAD

This salad comes from the hill villages of Tuscany where it is served as a mid-morning snack but it makes a good light lunch or it can be served as part of a salad buffet. In Italy the cheese is always Pecorino ewe's milk cheese, but you can use any kind of hard ewe's milk cheese. Choose a robust extra virgin olive oil as this is an important part of the flavour of the whole dish.

1 small ciabatta loaf or well flavoured white bread
1–2 cloves garlic, halved
8–10 tbsp extra virgin olive oil
2 handfuls rocket
2 handfuls baby spinach leaves
leaves from 1 small head red radicchio
175g Pecorino or hard vegetarian ewe's milk cheese, diced
4 tbsp walnut halves, coarsely chopped
small bunch parsley, freshly chopped

1. Cut the bread into four thick slices and rub each side with garlic. Brush all over with 2 tablespoons of olive oil and toast until it is lightly seared. Leave to cool.
2. Dice the bread and toss with the rocket, spinach and radicchio leaves. Add the cheese, walnuts and parsley.
3. Spoon the salad into individual bowls and pour over the rest of the olive oil. The quantity is up to you, but use at least one tablespoon per person.

CHAPTER 6
SNACKS AND SUPPER DISHES

Most of the dishes in this chapter are even faster to prepare than those in the rest of the book. Snack recipes are designed for occasions when all you have time for is a quick dash to the store cupboard or fridge and the bare minimum of preparation and cooking. The dishes are both filling and nutritious and do not need much in the way of accompaniments.

Many of these snacks are based on bread of various types. Wholemeal, granary and white breads all toast well, and you can also toast sourdough and rye breads for a more robust flavour and Italian-style ciabatta bread to make bruschetta with various toppings. French bread and pitta bread lend themselves to a variety of fillings. Some of these dishes can be made in advance for lunchboxes. Others can be cut into smaller portions and served as finger food at parties.

Eggs make a very good base for light supper dishes. Start in the American style with a small salad and finish with a plate of fresh or dried fruit. All recipes are for four people.

ANGLO-FRENCH BAGUETTE

The Cheshire town of Stalybridge is twinned with the French town of Armentières and this recipe celebrates the connection.

2 small baguettes (about 20–23cm long)
225g Appleby's Cheshire cheese, grated
1 hard-boiled egg, chopped
4 cocktail gherkins, chopped
4 stuffed olives, chopped
1 tsp chopped fresh chives
½ tsp French mustard
2 tbsp mayonnaise
salt and freshly ground black pepper
a few lettuce leaves

1. Cut the baguettes in half lengthways and hollow out slightly by removing some of the dough.
2. Place all the remaining ingredients except the lettuce in a bowl and mix well together.
3. Line the tops and bottoms of the baguettes with lettuce leaves. Spread the cheese mixture along the bottoms and cover with the lettuce-lined tops.
4. Squeeze together with your hands. Slice into 2.5cm lengths to serve.

SPICY CHEESE BOATS

When they are lined up on the serving dish these snacks look just like a boat marina – hence the name! They make a filling snack at any time of the day, but they can also be sliced and served as finger food at a drinks party. Use mature cheese to give a good robust flavour.

150ml mayonnaise
150g hard cheese such as mature Cheddar, finely grated
8–10 spring onions, finely chopped
2 tbsp chopped fresh basil
**1 tbsp soy sauce with chilli or ordinary soy sauce with a few
   drops of Tabasco sauce**
plenty of freshly ground black pepper
2 small baguettes (about 20–23cm long)

Garnish
sprigs of basil

1. Preheat the oven to 180°C/Gas 4.
2. Mix the mayonnaise in a bowl with the cheese, spring onions, basil, soy sauce and black pepper.
3. Cut the baguettes in half lengthways and spread the cut sides with the cheese mixture.
4. Place on a baking sheet and bake for 10–15 minutes until lightly browned on top. Serve garnished with sprigs of basil.

VARIATIONS

Slice two tomatoes and arrange on top of the baguettes before spreading on the cheese mixture. Alternatively use one tomato and arrange on two baguette halves, leaving the other two without tomato.

BRUSCHETTA WITH MUSHROOMS (V)

This is a variation on the usual bruschetta made with tomatoes, garlic and olive oil.

6 tbsp extra virgin olive oil, plus extra for drizzling
2–3 garlic cloves, crushed
4 large flat mushrooms
salt and freshly ground black pepper
4 thick slices of ciabatta bread
1 large tomato, thinly sliced
6 spring onions, thinly sliced
1 tsp dried oregano

1. Preheat the grill. Put the olive oil and garlic in a small saucepan over a low heat until the garlic is very lightly browned. Brush the mushrooms all over with the mixture, then season

2. Place the mushrooms under the hot grill, turning once, until cooked through.

3. Meanwhile, brush the remaining garlic and oil mixture over both sides of each slice of bread. Place the slices under the grill until lightly browned on both sides.

4. Top each piece of bread with a cooked mushroom and slices of tomato. Return to the grill for 2 minutes.

5. Finally, top with the spring onions and oregano, drizzle a little more olive oil over the bruschetta and return to the grill for 2 minutes. Serve at once.

VARIATION
Non-vegans might like to add a thin slice of cheese on top of the tomato.

CLASSIC WELSH RAREBIT

This is a really delicious Welsh rarebit and I can eat two rounds at a sitting! However, this quantity will serve four people for a quick snack.

25g butter
25g plain flour
200ml beer (ale or lager)
100ml skimmed milk
125g Cheddar cheese, grated
½–1 tsp mustard powder or made mustard
cayenne pepper
4 large slices of wholemeal bread

Optional flavourings
1 tbsp capers, chopped
1 tbsp gherkins, chopped
1 tbsp walnuts, chopped

1. Preheat the grill to medium. Put the butter, flour, beer and milk in a saucepan. Bring to the boil over a low heat, whisking all the time with a wire whisk.
2. When the mixture boils and thickens, cook for a further minute. Add the cheese, mustard, cayenne pepper to taste and any or all of the optional flavourings.
3. Toast the bread lightly on both sides. Spread one side generously with the cheese mixture and grill for 4–5 minutes until browned. Serve hot.

VARIATION

To make a more substantial snack add a fried egg on top of each slice of toast.

SPICY CHEESE ON TOAST

Very often the simplest foods are the tastiest and this is certainly true of this lightly curried cheesy topping for toast. Any kind of chutney can be used here.

125g Cheddar cheese, grated
2 tbsp ginger chutney
1 tsp mild curry powder
4 large slices of wholemeal bread
4 tomatoes, sliced

1. Preheat the grill to hot. Mix the cheese, chutney and curry powder to a thick paste.
2. Toast the bread lightly on both sides. Top each slice with tomatoes.
3. Spread the cheese mixture over the top and grill for 3–4 minutes until the cheese is bubbling. Serve hot.

CHEESE AND SALSA TOASTS

I love cheese on toast in any shape or form. This version uses a Mexican-style salsa to give a spicy finish. If you have the time, make a double quantity of the salsa and store in the fridge to use with stuffed taco shells or grilled vegetables.

4 thick slices of country bread or ciabatta, or French bread sliced open lengthways
4 tbsp extra virgin olive oil
175g mature Cheddar cheese, grated

Salsa
2 tomatoes, skinned and finely chopped
1 fresh green chilli, seeded and chopped
½ bunch of spring onions, finely chopped
½ small pickled cucumber, finely chopped
1 garlic clove, peeled and finely chopped (optional)
3 tbsp chopped fresh parsley, basil, coriander or tarragon

1. Start by making the salsa. Mix all the ingredients in a bowl and leave to stand until required.
2. Preheat the grill. Brush the bread on both sides with a little olive oil and toast both sides.
3. Spread the grated cheese over each slice, taking the cheese to the edge of the bread. Spoon the salsa down the middle. Place under the grill and serve as soon as the cheese starts to bubble.

GARLIC TOASTS WITH TOMATO SALSA (V)

This recipe is guaranteed to give even unripe winter tomatoes a touch of Mexican sunshine! Serve as a snack on sliced French bread or cut the bread into rounds and serve at a finger buffet.

2 small baguettes (about 20–23cm long)
1 garlic clove, peeled and cut in half
4 tbsp extra virgin olive oil

Salsa
6–8 tomatoes, skinned and diced
1 small bunch of spring onions, chopped
1 fresh green chilli, seeded and chopped
6 tbsp chopped fresh coriander
juice of ½ a lemon
freshly ground black pepper

1. Preheat the grill. Cut the baguettes in half lengthways. Rub all over with the clove of garlic and brush with some of the olive oil. Place under a hot grill until lightly browned on both sides.

2. Meanwhile, mix all the salsa ingredients in a bowl. Spread the salsa over the cut side of each baguette. Grill for 2–3 minutes. Drizzle with the remaining olive oil. Cut each baguette in half and serve at once.

VARIATION

Use lime juice in place of the lemon juice and add a little grated fresh root ginger to the salsa.

CURRIED BANANA TOASTS (V)

This banana mixture can be used cold to make open or closed sandwiches, but when it is grilled it takes on a new dimension. It is also very successful when cooked in a toasted sandwich machine. You can use a block of dried dates or the softer dates that come in boxes. The latter are easier to mash but they need to be stoned, so you will need to start with rather more of them: about 250g should be enough. Serve whole slices of toast as a substantial snack or cut into four squares to serve as finger food.

4 large slices of wholemeal bread
4 large bananas, peeled
a little grated lemon zest
2 tbsp mango chutney
175g dried dates, chopped and mashed
1 tsp curry powder
salt and freshly ground black pepper

1. Preheat the grill. Toast the bread well on one side and lightly on the second side.
2. Mash the bananas with a fork and immediately mix with the lemon zest and chutney. Then mix in the dates, curry powder, salt and pepper to make a thick paste. Spread this mixture on the lightly toasted side of the bread and place under a hot grill for about 5 minutes until the mixture bubbles; serve at once.

VARIATION

Top with grated cheese. Allow about 125g for four slices of toast. Sprinkle over the banana mixture when it has been under the grill for about 3 minutes.

MUSHROOM AND CHEESE SAUTÉ

The inspiration for this rich and warming snack comes from the Austrian Alps, where wild mushrooms abound. Unfortunately, most Austrian cheeses are made with rennet, so choose a hard cheese such as Appleby's Double Gloucester or the French Abbaye de Belloc instead. The mixture also makes a good topping for canapés: a double quantity will be sufficient for twelve slices of toasted French bread.

30 dried wild mushrooms
50g butter
2 tbsp extra virgin olive oil
400g button mushrooms, thinly sliced
2 tbsp brandy
4 thick slices of ciabatta bread
6 tbsp grated hard cheese
a pinch of freshly grated nutmeg
salt and freshly ground black pepper
4 large sprigs of flat-leaf parsley

1. Put the dried mushrooms in a small bowl and add boiling water to barely cover. Leave to stand for 15 minutes.
2. Meanwhile, heat the butter and olive oil in a small frying pan over a low heat and add the fresh mushrooms. Sauté gently for 5 minutes.
3. Add the soaked mushrooms and their liquid to the fresh mushrooms and bring to the boil. Add the brandy and cook over a high heat for about 3–4 minutes until all the liquid has evaporated.
4. Toast the bread until seared on both sides.
5. Add 2 tablespoons of the cheese, the nutmeg, salt and pepper to the mushroom mixture. Pile onto the prepared toast. Sprinkle with the remaining cheese and decorate with a large sprig of flat-leaf parsley. Serve at once.

TOFU SESAME SLICES (V)

The longer you are able to marinate the tofu the better it will taste. Serve on a bed of peppery leaves such as rocket or watercress. If you want a more substantial supper dish add a helping of Warm Spicy Noodle Salad (page 214).

300g firm tofu
2 tbsp dark soy sauce
juice of ½ lemon
2 tbsp grated fresh root ginger
1 garlic clove, peeled and cut in half
2 tbsp plain flour
4 tbsp sesame seeds
5 tbsp extra virgin olive or groundnut oil
salad leaves such as rocket, to serve

1. Cut the tofu into eight strips and place in a shallow dish.
2. Mix the soy sauce, lemon juice and ginger and pour over the tofu. Add the pieces of garlic to the marinade and leave to stand until required.
3. Mix the flour and sesame seeds on a plate. Dip the marinated tofu slices into the mixture and coat well on both sides.
4. Heat 2 tablespoons of the oil in a frying pan over a medium–high heat and fry the coated tofu on both sides until lightly browned and crisp. This will only take about 1 minute on each side.
5. Arrange the salad leaves on individual plates and transfer the tofu slices to the plates, using a fish slice.
6. Mix any remaining marinade with the rest of the olive oil and spoon over the top. Serve at once.

LA MANCHA-STYLE STEWED VEGETABLES WITH EGGS

This authentic Spanish recipe is similar to the French ratatouille but does not include aubergines, and eggs are added. Serve with hunks of crusty bread.

3 tbsp extra virgin olive oil
½ onion, peeled and chopped
1 garlic clove, peeled and crushed
2 green peppers, seeded and chopped
1 red pepper, seeded and chopped
450g tomatoes
450g courgettes, chopped
salt and freshly ground black pepper
3 eggs, beaten

1. Heat the oil in a saucepan over a low heat and fry the onion and garlic until golden. Add the peppers, cover with a lid, and continue to cook gently while you prepare the tomatoes.

2. Put the tomatoes in a bowl, pour boiling water over them to loosen the skins, then peel, halve and remove the seeds and any hard parts. Add to the peppers, crushing with a wooden spoon. Cook uncovered over a low heat for about 6–8 minutes.

3. Before the liquid from the tomatoes has completely evaporated, add the courgettes to the pan. When the courgettes begin to soften, add the salt and pepper. Cook over a low heat for a few more minutes until the vegetables are just tender.

4. Add the beaten eggs and cook until set, stirring once or twice. Serve with crusty bread or toasted croutons.

WATERCRESS AND COTTAGE CHEESE OMELETTE

The cottage cheese provides a very light texture to this quickly made omelette and the watercress gives it a spicy flavour.

4 heaped tbsp cottage cheese
a little crushed garlic (optional)
½ bunch of watercress, coarsely chopped
2 tbsp freshly grated Parmesan-style cheese
6 eggs
6 tbsp water
salt and freshly ground black pepper
1 tbsp extra virgin olive oil

1. Mix the cottage cheese with the garlic (if using), watercress and grated cheese and keep on one side.
2. Beat the eggs with the water, salt and pepper.
3. Put a 20cm omelette pan over a medium–high heat, add the oil and swirl around the pan, then pour in the eggs; stir gently once or twice, then cook until lightly set.
4. Dot with spoonfuls of the cheese and watercress mixture. Fold up and serve at once.

IRANIAN OMELETTE
WITH COURGETTES AND MINT

Iranian omelettes are flat omelettes similar to Spanish tortilla but they are not cooked for so long and should be just a little runny in the centre. The yogurt makes them very light and fluffy.

225g courgettes, diced
6 eggs, beaten
4 tbsp natural yogurt
salt and freshly ground black pepper
2 tbsp chopped fresh mint
1 tbsp extra virgin olive oil

1. Steam the courgettes or boil in a very little water for 4 minutes until just tender or al dente.
2. Beat the eggs with the yogurt, salt, pepper and mint, and stir in the cooked courgettes.
3. Heat the oil in a small (about 20cm) frying pan and pour in the egg mixture.
4. Cook over a medium heat for 2 minutes, stir once or twice, then cook for a further 6–8 minutes until just set in the centre. Serve from the pan.

VARIATIONS

In place of courgettes and mint, you could make this with peas and freshly chopped chervil, diced celeriac and chopped chives or spring onions and chopped sage.

SOUFFLÉ OMELETTE
WITH SPINACH AND PINE NUTS

An Italian-inspired dish: 'Florentine' dishes are often made with spinach, and in Rome spinach is often cooked with pine nuts and raisins.

1 tbsp butter
2 tbsp pine nuts
2 tbsp raisins
450g young spinach leaves
a little grated lemon zest
6 eggs, separated
4 tbsp water
salt and freshly ground black pepper

1. Heat the butter in a saucepan over a low heat and gently fry the pine nuts and raisins until the nuts begin to brown. Add the spinach and toss until the leaves begin to wilt. Chop coarsely, add the lemon zest and leave to cool.
2. Beat the egg yolks with the water, salt and pepper and stir into the spinach.
3. Whisk the egg whites until they are stiff. Stir a tablespoonful into the yolk and spinach mixture and then fold in the rest.
4. Preheat the grill. Lightly oil a non-stick 25cm frying pan and place over a low heat. Pour in the spinach mixture and cook for 4–5 minutes.
5. Place the pan under the grill – not too hot – and cook for 5 minutes until set in the centre. Serve from the pan.

ASPARAGUS AND SWEETCORN OMELETTE

For quick cooking use the largest frying pan you have. This allows all the ingredients to spread out into a set omelette about 1cm thick. If the mixture is too thick it will take longer to cook.

2 large potatoes, peeled and cut into chunks
2 tbsp extra virgin olive oil
2 onions, peeled and thinly sliced
225g cooked or canned sweetcorn
425g can asparagus spears, drained and chopped
6 eggs
salt and freshly ground black pepper

1. Cook the potatoes in boiling water for about 10 minutes until just tender. Drain and cut into dice.
2. Heat the oil in a large frying pan over a medium heat and fry the onions for 3–4 minutes until lightly browned. Add the sweetcorn, asparagus and diced potatoes.
3. Preheat the grill to high.
4. Beat the eggs with the salt and pepper and pour over the vegetables. Cook over a medium heat for about 5 minutes until the base is well browned. Place the pan under the grill until the top has set. Serve at once.

VARIATION

Top with a little grated cheese before the omelette goes under the grill.

SOUFFLÉ OMELETTE
WITH STIR-FRIED VEGETABLES

It does not take very long to whisk up this frothy omelette and the filling can be varied according to the contents of your vegetable rack. For a more substantial supper, serve with boiled new potatoes.

6 eggs, separated
3 tbsp water
salt and freshly ground black pepper

Filling
½ green pepper, seeded and cut into thin strips
½ red pepper, seeded and cut into thin strips
50g mangetout or green beans, stringed
1 tbsp groundnut oil
50g bean sprouts
1 tsp soy sauce

1. Prepare all the vegetables for the filling. Heat the oil in a wok or deep frying pan over a high heat and stir-fry the peppers and mangetout or beans for 2 minutes. Keep on one side.
2. Beat the egg yolks with the water, salt and pepper. Whisk the egg whites until they are stiff. Stir a tablespoonful into the yolks and then fold in the rest.
3. Preheat the grill. Lightly oil a 25cm frying pan and place over a medium heat. Pour in the egg mixture and cook for about 6 minutes until the omelette is just set and the base is lightly browned.
4. Place the pan under the grill – not too hot – and cook for 4–5 minutes or until set in the centre.
5. Add the bean sprouts and soy sauce to the stir-fried vegetables and put over a high heat for a minute. Toss well together and spoon onto the omelette. Fold over and serve at once.

SWEETCORN AND POTATO FRITTERS

This simple variation on the Jewish latkes is very quick to make when you are hungry. Serve with Yellow Tomato Salsa (see page 150).

900g potatoes, peeled and coarsely grated
175g canned or thawed frozen sweetcorn
2 eggs, beaten
salt and freshly ground black pepper
2–3 tbsp extra virgin olive oil

1. Gently squeeze the grated potatoes and drain off any liquid, then mix them with the sweetcorn, eggs, salt and pepper.
2. Heat the oil in a large heavy-based frying pan and drop tablespoonfuls of the mixture into it. Cook the fritters over a low–medium heat for about 5–6 minutes on each side until crisp and golden; you may need to cook them in batches. Check that the potato in the centre is fully cooked before serving.

CELERIAC TORTILLA WITH MUSHROOMS

A tortilla makes a satisfying snack. You can eat it hot as soon as it is cooked, or you can leave it to cool and finish it later. Add a tomato salad and a hunk of bread and the snack becomes a meal.

3 tbsp extra virgin olive oil
½ celeriac (approx. 250g), peeled and finely diced
1 potato, peeled and finely diced
1 onion, peeled and diced
175g chestnut mushrooms, wiped and sliced
7 eggs, beaten
2 tbsp chopped fresh parsley
salt and freshly ground black pepper

1. Heat the oil in a 20–23cm frying pan over a medium heat and gently fry the celeriac, potato and onion for about 10 minutes, turning from time to time, until the vegetables are softened but not browned.
2. Stir in the mushrooms and fry for a further minute or two until the mushrooms soften.
3. Beat the eggs with the parsley, salt and pepper and pour over the vegetables. Stir and leave to cook over a low heat for 5–6 minutes until the base is cooked.
4. Turn the tortilla over by placing a large plate over the pan and inverting the tortilla onto it. Slide the tortilla back into the pan to cook on the other side. This will take about another 5–6 minutes. Check that the vegetables are cooked through. Slide onto a warmed serving plate and cut into wedges to serve.

POTATO TORTILLA
WITH CREAMED SPINACH

I have been making this simple tortilla for many years and it is still a favourite with all the family. I make no apology for the fact that it appeared in my very first vegetarian cookbook (though in none since) because I hope that a new generation of cooks will enjoy it as much as we do! The dish stands on its own, but if you have time it is very good served with Grilled Vegetables with Pesto Mayonnaise (see page 146).

750g potatoes, peeled and grated
1 large onion, very finely chopped
3 eggs, beaten
1 tbsp plain flour
½ tsp dried mixed herbs
salt and freshly ground black pepper
2 tbsp extra virgin olive oil

Creamed spinach
450g frozen chopped spinach
125g full-fat soft cheese, cut into small pieces
6 tbsp double cream
a pinch of freshly grated nutmeg
salt and freshly ground black pepper

1. Gently squeeze the grated potatoes and drain off any liquid, then mix them with the onion, eggs, flour, herbs, salt and pepper.

2. Heat the oil in a 20–23cm non-stick frying pan over a medium heat. Spoon in the potato and onion mixture and spread evenly over the base of the pan. Cook for about 10–15 minutes, depending on the thickness of the tortilla.

3. When the base is well browned, turn the tortilla over by placing a large plate over the pan and inverting the tortilla onto it. Slide the tortilla back into the pan to cook on the other side for another 10–15 minutes.

4. Meanwhile, put the spinach in a saucepan over a low heat to thaw. Add the cheese and the cream. Stir until all the cheese has melted and mixed into the spinach. Add nutmeg, salt and pepper to taste and bring to the boil.

5. Turn the tortilla out onto a serving plate and cut into wedges to serve, with the creamed spinach on the side.

AVOCADO, TOMATO AND CORIANDER IN TACO SHELLS (V)

This mixture is rather like a chunky version of guacamole. It makes a really good snack served in warm taco shells.

4 large taco shells or 8 smaller ones
1 ripe avocado, peeled, stoned and diced
2 tomatoes, skinned, seeded and diced
5 small spring onions, finely chopped
1 garlic clove, peeled and crushed
4 tbsp chopped fresh coriander
juice of 1 lemon
salt and freshly ground black pepper

Garnish
4 sprigs of coriander

1. Preheat the oven as directed on the pack of taco shells and follow the instructions for heating them through.
2. Mix all the remaining ingredients together in a bowl.
3. Pile the mixture into the taco shells and garnish with sprigs of coriander.

TACO SHELLS WITH CAULIFLOWER AND GUACAMOLE (V)

Most shops now sell ready-made guacamole and pickled beetroot, so this is a very quick snack to make. If you like really spicy food you can pep up the guacamole with some finely chopped chilli.

4 large taco shells or 8 smaller ones
1 small cauliflower (approx. 500g), cut into florets
2 tbsp extra virgin olive oil
½ iceberg lettuce, shredded
150g guacamole
100g pickled beetroot, drained and chopped

1. Preheat the oven as directed on the pack of taco shells and follow the instructions for heating them through.
2. Place the cauliflower florets in a steamer over a pan of boiling water, cover with a lid and cook for 6–8 minutes. There should still be a bit of a bite to the cauliflower.
3. Cut the cauliflower into smaller pieces and toss with the oil.
4. Remove the taco shells from the oven and fill each one with a little shredded lettuce. Then add the dressed cauliflower. Top with a spoonful of guacamole and some chopped beetroot. Serve at once.

VARIATIONS

Use hummus instead of guacamole and mix with freshly chopped coriander.

Top with chopped capers mixed with toasted pine nuts instead of pickled beetroot.

GRILLED GEM LETTUCES WITH PEPPERS AND GOAT'S CHEESE IN PITTA PARCELS

This is a fresh twist on the traditional pitta breads filled with falafel and hummus.

Any log-shaped goat's cheese can be used.

4 Little Gem lettuces
4–5 tbsp extra virgin olive oil
2 large red peppers, seeded and cut into large pieces
4 pitta breads
salt and freshly ground black pepper
225g log-shaped goat's cheese, cut into four slices
sprigs of basil

1. Preheat the grill to hot. Brush the lettuces with plenty of olive oil and cook under the hot grill until they are lightly seared on one side. Turn over, brush with more oil and cook until the other side is lightly browned. Remove from the heat and keep on one side.
2. Place the pieces of red pepper skin-side up under the grill and cook until well browned. Remove from the heat and leave to cool a little. If you like you can remove the charred skin.
3. Lightly toast the pitta breads under the grill. Split open and brush the insides with olive oil. Sprinkle with salt and pepper.
4. Fill the pitta breads with the grilled vegetables and a slice of goat's cheese. Add a few sprigs of basil and serve at once.

CHAPTER 7
CASSEROLES, CURRIES AND STOVETOP DISHES

Casseroles are often associated with long slow cooking in the oven but it is not necessary to use the oven to achieve a good depth of flavour in this type of dish. Indian curries and African tagines, for example, are traditionally cooked on the top of the stove and they are certainly not lacking in flavour. Nor is it necessary to cook the vegetables for a long time. However, it does makes sense to use a medium rather than a low heat to ensure that ingredients are fully cooked in half an hour. Stir from time to time to make sure that the casserole or curry does not stick to the pan. If the juices are still rather runny after this time, turn up the heat to reduce and concentrate the sauce in the last five minutes of cooking time.

In addition to casseroles and curries I have included some other dishes which can be cooked on the top of the stove, such as some hearty vegetable pancakes. There is also a recipe for casserole dumplings; if you do want to add dumplings to a dish you may like to use slightly more stock than given in the recipe.

All the recipes in this chapter are for four people. Some dishes are complete meals by themselves, others will need an accompaniment of rice, noodles, potatoes, couscous or bulgur wheat. Alternatively, choose two of these dishes to serve together.

CHICKPEAS WITH SPINACH (V)

Chickpeas, or garbanzo beans as they are known in Spain, are very popular in the tapas bars of Seville. This dish is usually served in an oval dish surrounded by triangles of bread fried in olive oil.

2 tbsp extra virgin olive oil
1 garlic clove, peeled and crushed
1 small onion, peeled and chopped
a few strands of saffron
3 tomatoes, skinned, seeded and chopped
400g can chickpeas, drained
450g fresh spinach, shredded

1. Heat the olive oil in a saucepan and gently fry the garlic and onion until softened. Add the saffron and cook for a minute. Add the tomatoes and cook for 2–3 minutes, stirring from time to time, until thick. Add the chickpeas and mix well.
2. Put the spinach in a saucepan (with no added water), cover with a lid and place over a medium–high heat for 1–2 minutes until it is just wilted.
3. Toss the spinach with the chickpeas and spoon into a serving bowl.

MOROCCAN TAGINE OF SWISS CHARD (V)

Tagine is a North African word for stew. It is also the name of the earthenware dish in which stews are often cooked; it has a conical lid with a small hole in the top to let out the steam. But you can cook a tagine just as well in a saucepan. All kinds of ingredients find their way into a tagine: this version uses Swiss chard. If you can't find Swiss chard you can use spring greens or large garden spinach leaves. This is often served with a dish of stewed lentils.

1kg Swiss chard
2 onions, peeled and chopped
4 tbsp chopped fresh coriander
3 tbsp long-grain rice
6 tbsp vegetable stock or water
4 tbsp extra virgin olive oil
1 tsp paprika
salt and freshly ground black pepper

1. Wash the Swiss chard and dry well on kitchen paper. Chop the stalks finely and tear the leaves into shreds.
2. Place all the ingredients in a heavy-based saucepan over a high heat and bring to the boil.
3. Reduce the heat, cover with a lid and simmer for 12–15 minutes until the vegetables and rice are cooked and the mixture is thick. Serve hot.

TAGINE OF OKRA AND TOMATOES (V)

Choose small okra for this dish from Morocco. Take care not to overcook okra, as this vegetable can be very glutinous and stringy if it starts to break up. Serve with rice.

1kg fresh ripe tomatoes, skinned, seeded and chopped
2 tbsp chopped fresh parsley
2 tsp paprika
1 garlic clove, peeled and crushed
salt and freshly ground black pepper
3 tbsp extra virgin olive oil
225g fresh or frozen very small or baby okra

1. Place all the ingredients except the okra in a heavy-based saucepan over a high heat. Bring to the boil and cook for 10 minutes, stirring all the time until the tomatoes have broken down and the mixture is fairly thick.
2. Reduce the heat and add the okra, pushing it well down into the sauce. Cover with a lid and simmer for 10 minutes until the okra is cooked through. Serve hot.

ALGERIAN-STYLE EGGS

In North Africa eggs are rarely served in restaurants, but they are used in the home and hard-boiled eggs with cumin are sold as street snacks. This recipe comes from Algeria and can be served with couscous or bulgur wheat, or with quinoa.

6 eggs
1 garlic clove, cut in half
2 tbsp extra virgin olive oil
450g tomatoes, skinned, seeded and chopped
3 shallots or ½ small onion, peeled and finely chopped
salt and freshly ground black pepper
¼ tsp ground cumin

1. Cook two of the eggs in boiling water for 10 minutes. Drain and cover with very cold water until cool enough to handle, then peel and roughly chop.
2. Meanwhile, rub a small heavy-based pan with the garlic. Add the olive oil, tomatoes and shallots or onion and cook over a medium heat for 15 minutes, stirring from time to time until the mixture is thick.
3. Beat the remaining eggs and add to the tomato mixture with the salt, pepper and cumin. Stir and gently scramble for 2–3 minutes until not quite set.
4. Add the chopped eggs and cook for a further minute. Serve at once or the mixture will harden.

CURRIED BEANS

This straightforward curry is fairly mild, so if you like your curries hot add a dash or two of Tabasco. Serve with potatoes sautéed with cardamom, or spiced rice.

5cm piece of fresh root ginger, peeled and chopped
3 large garlic cloves, peeled and chopped
1 large onion, peeled and chopped
3 tbsp groundnut oil
1 tsp cumin seeds
1 tsp coriander seeds
seeds from 4 cardamom pods
2 cloves
1 tbsp ground cumin
2 tsp ground coriander
400g can black-eyed beans, drained
200g can butter beans, drained
225g runner or flat green beans, stringed and sliced
2 tbsp ground almonds
150g natural yogurt
150ml vegetable stock or water

1. Finely chop the ginger, garlic and onion in a food processor or blender and keep on one side.
2. Heat the oil in a saucepan over a medium heat and fry the whole spices for about 1 minute until they start to pop. Take care not to burn them.
3. Remove from the heat and stir in the ground spices and then the ginger mixture.
4. Return to the heat and add all the remaining ingredients. Stir well and bring to the boil. Reduce the heat, cover with a lid and simmer for 15 minutes. Serve hot.

VARIATION

Use soya yogurt instead of cow's milk yogurt for a vegan curry.

MUSHROOM GOULASH WITH NOODLES (V)

For the best results, use a mixture of medium-sized chestnut mushrooms and small closed-cap mushrooms. However, you can make the goulash with just one type of mushroom. Goulash is traditionally made with soured cream, but the vegan version, with puréed tofu, is just as good.

2 tbsp extra virgin olive oil
1 large leek, trimmed and sliced
1 green pepper, seeded and chopped
2 tbsp paprika
450g closed-cap mushrooms, thickly sliced
175g chestnut mushrooms, thickly sliced
150ml vegetable stock
3 tbsp tomato purée
4 tbsp chopped fresh parsley
salt and freshly ground black pepper
225g flat noodles, such as tagliatelle
3 tbsp soured cream or puréed silken tofu

1. Heat the oil in a saucepan and gently fry the leek and green pepper for 2 minutes. Stir in the paprika and cook for another minute or so.
2. Stir in the mushrooms, cover with a lid and cook gently for 5 minutes, stirring occasionally. Add the stock, tomato purée, half the parsley and the seasoning. Cook uncovered for 10 minutes.
3. Meanwhile, cook the noodles in plenty of salted boiling water for about 8–10 minutes or as directed on the pack.
4. Stir the soured cream or puréed tofu into the goulash and reheat. Drain the noodles thoroughly and pile onto serving plates. Top with the goulash and garnish with the remaining parsley.

CELERIAC WITH YOGURT AND POTATOES

I like this dish because the vegetables cook together into a wonderfully flavourful mass. Serve with a crunchy salad such as Watercress and Pistachio Salad (see page 80) or Hungarian Salad (see page 81).

1 tbsp extra virgin olive oil
1 onion, peeled and sliced
450g celeriac, peeled and finely diced
200g carrots, peeled and finely diced
350g potatoes, peeled and diced
¼ green pepper, seeded and chopped
4 tbsp natural yogurt
2 tbsp vegetable stock
salt and freshly ground black pepper

1. Heat the oil in a saucepan and gently fry the onion for a minute or two. Add the celeriac and carrots and cook gently for 3–4 minutes, stirring from time to time.
2. Add all the remaining ingredients and bring to the boil. Reduce the heat and cover with a lid. Simmer for about 15 minutes, stirring regularly.
3. Check to see if the vegetables are all cooked through: they may need another 5 minutes. Serve hot.

VARIATIONS

Stir in freshly chopped herbs just before serving.

Use 3 tablespoons frozen peas or broad beans in place of the green pepper.

INDIAN VEGETABLE CASSEROLE WITH OKRA (V)

The vegetables are cooked in coconut milk with southern Indian spicing. Serve with rice, quinoa or noodles.

3 tbsp groundnut oil
2 large onions, peeled and roughly chopped
2 large garlic cloves, peeled and chopped
2 tsp grated fresh root ginger
2 tsp mild curry powder
3 carrots, peeled and cut into thick rounds
175g green beans, trimmed and cut into 4cm lengths
175g baby sweetcorn
400ml can coconut milk
75ml vegetable stock
1 small bunch of coriander (about 20g), chopped
salt and freshly ground black pepper
225g fresh or frozen very small or baby okra

1. Heat the oil in a saucepan and gently fry the onions, garlic and ginger for about 3–4 minutes until softened but not browned.
2. Stir in the curry powder. Add the carrots, beans, sweetcorn, coconut milk, stock, half the coriander and the salt and pepper. Bring the mixture to the boil. Cook uncovered over a medium heat for about 15 minutes.
3. Add the okra and boil for 5 minutes until all the vegetables are tender and the sauce has thickened. Serve sprinkled with the remaining coriander.

MIXED ROOT VEGETABLE CURRY (V)

You can use any combination of three or four different root vegetables in this simple curry from northern India. However, parsnips give a distinctive flavour so go easy on these. To ensure that the dish cooks quickly, cut the vegetables into very small dice.

2 tbsp groundnut oil
½ tsp cumin seeds
seeds from 4 cardamom pods
¼ tsp fennel seeds (optional)
1 large onion, peeled and very finely chopped
2 garlic cloves, peeled and crushed
1 tbsp grated fresh root ginger
1 fresh green or red chilli, seeded and finely chopped
1kg mixed root vegetables (such as carrots, celeriac, Jerusalem
   artichokes, mooli/daikon, parsnips, swede or turnips),
   peeled and diced
1 large potato, peeled and diced
400ml tomato juice
salt and freshly ground black pepper

Garnish
2 tbsp flaked almonds or pine nuts, fried

1. Heat the oil in a deep heavy-based saucepan over a medium heat and fry the spices for about 1 minute. Remove from the heat if they start to smoke. Stir in the onion, garlic and ginger and fry for another minute or two.
2. Stir in the remaining ingredients and bring the mixture to the boil. Cover with a lid, reduce the heat and cook for 15–20 minutes, stirring from time to time until the vegetables are tender. Serve hot, sprinkled with the fried nuts.

VARIATIONS
Non-vegans might like to replace a third of the tomato juice with yogurt or single cream. Cream gives a silky rich texture and flavour to the dish.

CURRIED GREEN BANANAS WITH EGGS

If you live near a West Indian shop you should be able to find green bananas. Otherwise, the easiest way to make this dish is to buy dessert bananas while they are still green. These are not difficult to find when most fruit coming into the supermarkets is unripe! If you cannot find any kind of green bananas you can use ordinary bananas but you will need to reduce the cooking time by at least half.

Serve this with boiled rice. If you prefer to leave out the eggs you can serve another curry or vegetable dish alongside.

1 tbsp groundnut oil
½ tsp cumin seeds
1 tbsp curry powder
4 green or unripe bananas, peeled and sliced
125ml canned coconut milk
salt and freshly ground black pepper
2 eggs, beaten

1. Heat the oil in a saucepan over a medium heat and fry the cumin seeds for about 1 minute. Stir in the curry powder and the sliced bananas. When the bananas are well coated with the spicy mixture, pour in the coconut milk, salt and pepper.
2. Bring to the boil, cover with a lid and simmer for about 20 minutes until the bananas are tender and the liquid has thickened. Stir in the beaten eggs and cook for 1–2 minutes, then serve at once.

PUMPKIN AND CHICKPEA COUSCOUS (V)

Couscous is one of the staple foods in North Africa. It is made of tiny pieces of semolina which are best steamed or cooked in the quick method given below. Check the instructions on the pack of couscous before you buy it to see if it is suitable for this method. This dish is traditionally served with a North African chilli sauce called harissa; this is now widely available.

225g couscous
250ml water
1 tsp salt
3–4 tbsp extra virgin olive oil

Sauce
2 tsp cumin seeds
2 tsp dried oregano
½ tsp ground cinnamon
4 tbsp groundnut oil
2 large onions, peeled and coarsely chopped
2 large garlic cloves, peeled and chopped
2 fresh green or red chillies
200g celery, chopped
500g pumpkin, peeled, seeded and chopped
400g can chickpeas, drained
500ml vegetable stock
salt and freshly ground black pepper
a little potato flour or cornflour, mixed with a little water
   (optional)

1. To make the sauce, toast the cumin seeds in a heavy-based saucepan until they begin to brown. Add the oregano and cinnamon and stir. Add the oil, onions and garlic and fry for 2–3 minutes until lightly browned. Add all the remaining sauce ingredients except the potato flour or cornflour and bring to the boil. Cover with a lid and simmer for 15–20 minutes, then remove the chillies.

2. Meanwhile, to prepare the couscous, put the water, salt and 1 tablespoon of the olive oil in a large heavy-based saucepan and bring to the boil. Remove from the heat and stir in the couscous. Leave to stand for 3 minutes.

3. Return the pan to the heat and stir in the rest of the olive oil. Cook over a low heat for 3 minutes, stirring all the time to stop the couscous from sticking to the pan. Turn off the heat, cover with a lid and leave to stand until required.

4. Check the sauce and, if you would like it thicker, stir in the potato flour or cornflour and bring to the boil. Cook for 1 minute, then serve over the couscous.

LENTIL AND VEGETABLE STEW (V)

The lentils give this colourful vegetable stew a thick velvety sauce. The original recipe (without onions) came from the Gujarat area of India where much of the food is vegetarian. For a really authentic flavour leave out the onion and spices and use a Gujarati masala paste instead. Serve with boiled rice.

2 tbsp groundnut oil
½ tsp cumin seeds
½ tsp fenugreek or black mustard seeds (optional)
1 onion, peeled and finely chopped
1 green chilli, seeded and finely chopped
1 tbsp grated fresh root ginger
1 tsp turmeric
125g red or yellow split lentils
1 large carrot (approx. 175g), peeled and sliced into thin rounds
salt and freshly ground black pepper
200ml vegetable stock
2 large courgettes or winter squash (approx. 300g), sliced into rounds
4 tomatoes, coarsely chopped

1. Heat the oil in a large saucepan over a medium heat and fry the cumin and fenugreek or mustard seeds for 30 seconds. Add the onion, chilli, ginger and turmeric and fry for 2–3 minutes. Add the lentils and stir until they are well coated with the spicy mixture.
2. Add the carrot, salt, pepper and stock and bring to the boil. Cook uncovered over a medium heat for about 5–6 minutes.
3. Stir and add the courgettes and tomatoes. Bring back to the boil, then reduce the heat and simmer for about 10–15 minutes until the carrot is tender. Serve hot.

HARD-BOILED EGGS IN ONION SAUCE

I usually serve this old-fashioned French dish with plenty of crisp baguette, but it would also be good with boiled potatoes or large flat noodles tossed in butter and herbs. In the original recipe the onion sauce is rubbed through a sieve; today, it can be puréed in a blender. However, I rather like the texture of the onions in the sauce and I do not usually purée it.

6 large eggs
50g butter
450g onions, peeled and chopped
50g plain flour
1 tbsp chopped fresh tarragon or 1 tsp dried tarragon
a pinch of dried thyme
salt and freshly ground black pepper
600ml hot milk

1. Cook the eggs in boiling water for 10 minutes. Drain and cover with cold water until cool enough to handle.
2. Meanwhile, melt the butter in a saucepan and add the onions. Cook over a very low heat for about 8–10 minutes until the onions are soft; do not let them brown.
3. Using a wooden spoon, stir in the flour, herbs, salt and pepper until evenly mixed with the onions. Gradually add the milk and bring to the boil. Simmer for 3–4 minutes, stirring continuously.
4. Peel and slice or roughly chop the eggs and layer in a serving dish with the sauce. Serve at once.

VARIATION
Top the dish with 50g grated hard cheese mixed with 25g fresh breadcrumbs; brown under a hot grill.

SAG ALOO WITH GREENS (V)

In an Indian restaurant 'sag' usually means spinach, but it can also be translated as 'greens'. This recipe uses cabbage, kale or spring greens as well as spinach. Serve with Curried Green Bananas (see page 131), with or without the eggs, some chapatis and plain or lightly spiced yogurt with cucumber.

1 tbsp groundnut oil
½ tsp mustard seeds or cumin seeds
1 large garlic cloves, peeled and chopped
1 small onion, peeled and very finely chopped
1 tsp ground coriander
1 tsp ground turmeric
½–1 tsp chilli powder, according to taste
2 potatoes, peeled and diced
200g green cabbage, kale or spring greens, finely shredded
100ml vegetable stock
250g frozen chopped spinach

1. Heat the oil in a saucepan over a medium heat and fry the mustard or cumin seeds for 30 seconds. Add the garlic and onion and fry for 2–3 minutes.
2. Stir in the ground spices and then the potatoes, making sure that the potatoes are well coated with the spicy mixture. Add the greens and stock and bring to the boil. Cover with a lid and cook for about 10 minutes until the vegetables are almost tender.
3. Meanwhile, put the spinach in a small saucepan over a low heat to thaw. Stir from time to time.
4. When the vegetables are almost cooked, add the spinach and bring back to the boil. Reduce the heat and simmer for a further 5 minutes until the vegetables are fully cooked. Serve hot.

CURRIED CHESTNUTS (V)

You can buy cooked, peeled, unsweetened chestnuts in cans and in vacuum packs. They are ready to use and keep for a considerable time in the store cupboard.

This unusually sweet curry is very filling and you only need a small quantity. Serve with Mixed Root Vegetable Curry (see page 130) and boiled rice.

1 tbsp groundnut oil
1 onion, peeled and finely chopped
1 carrot, peeled and finely chopped
l garlic clove, peeled and crushed (optional)
1 tsp plain flour
1 tsp curry powder
300ml water
200g cooked, peeled chestnuts
25g raisins
1 tbsp mango chutney
1 tbsp cider vinegar

1. Heat the oil in a saucepan over a medium heat and fry the onion and carrot, and garlic if using, until they are lightly browned. Stir in the flour and curry powder and cook for another minute or so.
2. Gradually add the water, stirring all the time, and bring the mixture to the boil. Reduce the heat and add all the remaining ingredients. Cover with a lid and simmer for 15 minutes until all the vegetables are fully cooked. Serve hot.

HUNGARIAN CABBAGE PANCAKE

White cabbage would probably be the local choice for this dish from the Upper Danube, but I tried it with a firm green cabbage and the results were very good indeed. This pancake will serve four people as a side dish to accompany one of the casseroles in this section. Alternatively it would make a satisfying supper for two hungry people, served with stewed apples and some thick spiced yogurt.

400g cabbage, trimmed and very finely shredded
1 garlic clove, peeled
2 eggs
4 tbsp fresh breadcrumbs
½ tsp dried sage
salt and ground white pepper
2 tbsp extra virgin olive oil

1. Put the cabbage in a saucepan with the garlic. Cover with water and bring to the boil. Cook over a medium heat for about 10 minutes until the cabbage is tender. (If you have a little more time, cook the cabbage and garlic in a steamer.)

2. Drain the cabbage and dry on kitchen paper. Discard the garlic. Beat the eggs with the breadcrumbs, sage, salt and pepper and stir into the cabbage.

3. Preheat the grill. Heat the oil in an 18cm frying pan, and add the cabbage and egg mixture and spread out evenly. Fry for about 3–4 minutes until the base is browned. Place the pan under the grill to brown the top. Cut into wedges and serve.

VARIATIONS
Use 1 dessertspoon freshly chopped dill or a pinch of caraway seeds in place of the sage.

POTATO, CELERY AND SPINACH CAKE (V)

This fried vegetable cake is very satisfying on its own with a tomato and onion salad. Alternatively, for a more substantial supper, serve with another dish such as Hard-Boiled Eggs in Onion Sauce (see page 135) or Stuffed Marrow Rings (see pages 152–3).

4 medium to large potatoes, scrubbed
200g celery (2 large sticks), cut into 10cm lengths
350g fresh spinach
salt and freshly ground black pepper
4 tbsp extra virgin olive oil

1. Put the potatoes in their skins in a large saucepan, add the pieces of celery, pour in boiling water to cover and boil for about 5–6 minutes. Drain, peel the potatoes and dice finely. Chop the celery.
2. While the potatoes are cooking, wash the spinach, drain thoroughly and cook in a large saucepan (with no added water) over a low heat. Remove from the heat as soon as the leaves wilt. Drain off as much liquid as possible by pressing the leaves in a colander, then chop coarsely.
3. Mix all the vegetables in a large bowl and season well.
4. Heat the oil in a large frying pan. Pour half the oil over the vegetables and toss together. Spoon the mixture into the frying pan and cook over a medium heat for about 5–6 minutes until the base is well browned.
5. Put a plate over the pan and turn the vegetable cake onto it. Slide back into the pan to cook the other side for 5–6 minutes until browned. Slide onto a warmed plate to serve.

VARIATIONS
Non-vegans might like to use 50–75g butter in place of the oil; butter gives a quite different flavour to the dish. You can also sprinkle with grated smoked cheese just before serving.

BAKED RUTABAGA AND CARROT PUDDING

Rutabaga is the name the Americans give to the humble swede. I have deliberately used this transatlantic name to encourage you to look at the recipe and not turn over simply because it uses swede! This dish is both colourful and tasty and it makes an excellent main course with a couple of other vegetable dishes.

500g swede, peeled and very finely chopped
   or coarsely grated
approx. 500ml boiling vegetable stock
500g carrots, peeled and very finely chopped
   or coarsely grated
100ml double cream
3 tbsp chopped fresh chives
2–3 large sprigs of tarragon, chopped

1. Put the swede in a small saucepan and add boiling vegetable stock to just cover. Bring back to the boil and cook for 8–10 minutes until just tender.
2. Put the carrots in a small saucepan and add boiling vegetable stock to just cover. Bring back to the boil and cook for 6–7 minutes until just tender.

3. Drain the vegetables thoroughly, retaining the cooking liquid for use in stock or another recipe. Mash the swede with a fork or potato masher and stir in half the cream and all the chives. Mash the carrots and add the rest of the cream and the tarragon.

4. Spoon the carrot mixture into a pudding bowl and press well down. Top with the swede mixture and press well down again. Cover the bowl with clingfilm and place in a saucepan; add hot water to come about 3cm up the side of the bowl. Bring to the boil and simmer for 10 minutes. Turn out and serve hot.

VARIATION

Place a little sliced mature hard cheese between the two layers of vegetables.

ALMOND CASSEROLE DUMPLINGS

Vary the flavourings in these simple dumplings to complement the dish they are to accompany. For example, I use ground cumin for Indian Vegetable Casserole with Okra (see page 129). The mixture also makes very good dumplings for soup: shape into smaller balls and flavour with grated fresh ginger and finely chopped lemongrass, or with grated lime zest and chopped fresh coriander.

25g fresh wholemeal breadcrumbs
2 tbsp milk
25g ground almonds
1 small egg, beaten
50g self-raising flour
salt and freshly ground black pepper

Optional flavourings
1 tsp ground cumin
1 tbsp grated fresh root ginger
1 tsp grated lemon zest

1. Soak the breadcrumbs in the milk for 5–6 minutes. Add the almonds and egg and beat together. Stir in the flour, seasoning and your chosen flavouring, if desired.
2. Shape the mixture into 12 balls for casseroles and stews or about 16 balls for soup.
3. Drop all the dumplings into a large pan of boiling water. There should be enough room for them all to cook without touching too much. Bring the water back to the boil, then reduce the heat and simmer for 10–15 minutes (depending on size), turning the dumplings from time to time. Lift out with a slotted spoon and transfer to the casserole or soup.

VARIATION
Toast the ground almonds under the grill before using.

CABBAGE PARCELS
WITH SCRAMBLED EGGS

It is important to cook the cabbage leaves fully before scrambling the eggs for the filling; the dish is served as soon as the leaves are filled.

8 green cabbage or spring green leaves
450g carrots, peeled and grated
4 eggs
2 tbsp cold water
2 tsp dried tarragon
salt and freshly ground black pepper

1. Steam the cabbage or spring green leaves for about 15–20 minutes until tender.
2. Put the carrots in a small saucepan and add boiling water to just cover. Bring back to the boil and cook for about 5–6 minutes until tender. Drain well, retaining the carrot water for stock.
3. When the cabbage leaves are cooked, drain on kitchen paper while you scramble the eggs with the cold water until lightly set. Mix with the cooked carrots and tarragon, and season to taste.
4. Place 1 tablespoon of this mixture on the centre of each cooked cabbage leaf and fold up into a parcel. Serve at once.

VARIATIONS
Use kohlrabi and mint or parsnips and sage in place of carrots and tarragon.

GUJRATI-STYLE CAULIFLOWER (V)

In Gujrat many people do not eat onion or garlic, so the cuisine relies for its flavours on tamarind, mustard seed, chilli and coconut. It is possible to find tamarind in larger supermarkets and specialist shops, but I use a tamarind and date chutney which gives a very similar effect. Go easy on the mustard seed and chilli if you do not like dishes too hot as the chutney contains them both.

1 tbsp tamarind and date chutney
100ml water
2 tbsp peanut oil
1 tsp mustard seeds
1 cauliflower, broken into small florets
1 tsp ground turmeric
1 tsp ground chilli powder
Salt, to taste
2 tbsp desiccated coconut

1. Mix the chutney with the water and keep to one side
2. Heat the oil in a pan and fry the mustard seeds. Cover the pan with a lid while you do this or the seeds will pop out of the pan. Stop frying after a maximum of a minute or they will burn. Add the cauliflower and continue frying for 2-3 minutes.
3. Add chutney and water mix and all the remaining ingredients. Bring to the boil. Continue cooking over a low heat for 15 minutes until the cauliflower is just tender. Stir once or twice during this time.
4. If there is any liquid left in the bottom of the pan, quickly boil it off before serving.

CHAPTER 8
GRILLS AND BARBECUES

People often think that a vegetarian barbecue is difficult to manage, but most vegetables grill very well, particularly if they are brushed with olive oil or marinated first. The marinade can then be used for basting. You can also grill tofu or a cheese which does not melt easily such as feta or halloumi. The recipes in this section range from simple grilled vegetables partnered by interesting sauces to some unusual kebabs.

Most of these recipes can be cooked under the grill in the kitchen or over a barbecue. All recipes are for four people unless otherwise stated.

GRILLED VEGETABLES
WITH PESTO MAYONNAISE

Any kind of vegetables can be used in this recipe. Start with the
hardest and longest cooking and add the others to the grill as you
go along. If you are using a barbecue, transfer cooked vegetables
to the tray above the barbecue to keep warm. This makes
enough for four people as a starter or two as a main course.

2 sweet potatoes, scrubbed and sliced
1 large aubergine, sliced
2 tbsp extra virgin olive oil
1 large red pepper, seeded and cut into 8 pieces
2 large courgettes, sliced lengthways
4 tbsp mayonnaise
1–2 tsp pesto sauce
sprigs of chervil, tarragon or basil
sprigs of fresh flat-leaf parsley

1. Preheat the grill. Brush the sweet potatoes and aubergine
   slices on both sides with olive oil. Place on the grill rack and
   cook until lightly browned. Turn and cook the second side.
   Remove from the grill and keep warm.
2. Brush the pepper and courgettes with the remaining oil and
   place on the grill rack. Cook until the pepper is well charred.
   Turn the courgette slices over once.
3. Mix the mayonnaise and pesto together and keep on one side.
4. Arrange the cooked vegetables on serving plates, scatter the
   herbs on top and serve the pesto mayonnaise on the side.

VARIATION

As soon as the vegetables are cooked, arrange in a shallow dish and
drizzle with 2 tablespoons extra virgin olive oil and 1 tablespoon lemon
juice. Leave to stand for as long as possible before serving.

GRILLED AUBERGINES WITH MOROCCAN SAUCE (V)

The warmth of the grilled aubergines brings out the flavours of this piquant sauce from North Africa. Serve as a first course and follow with a tagine or couscous dish. Alternatively serve with rice, couscous or bulgur as a main course.

2 large aubergines, trimmed and thickly sliced
extra virgin olive oil for brushing

Moroccan sauce
3 tbsp extra virgin olive oil
1 garlic clove, crushed
1 tsp grated fresh root ginger
1 green chilli, seeded and chopped
½ tsp ground cumin
4 tbsp chopped fresh coriander
1 tbsp lemon juice
salt and freshly ground black pepper

1. Preheat the grill to medium-hot. Brush the aubergine slices on both sides with olive oil and grill for about 3–4 minutes on each side until lightly browned and cooked through.
2. To make the sauce, put all the ingredients in a food processor or blender (or use a hand-held blender) and mix together.
3. Arrange the aubergines on serving plates and spoon the sauce over the top. Serve at once.

GRILLED AUBERGINES
WITH OLIVE PASTE AND TOMATOES (V)

I prefer black olive paste to green olive paste for this flavourful aubergine dish from southern Italy. I sometimes add a slice of mozzarella or goat's cheese to each slice of aubergine just before removing from the grill.

2 aubergines, trimmed and cut into 16 thick slices
extra virgin olive oil for brushing
125g olive paste
4 tomatoes, each cut into 4 thick slices
freshly ground black pepper

1. Preheat the grill to medium-hot. Very lightly brush the aubergine slices on both sides with olive oil and grill for about 3–4 minutes on each side until golden brown and cooked through.
2. Spread each slice with some of the olive paste. Top with a slice of tomato and season with pepper. Return to the grill and cook for another 1–2 minutes. Serve at once.

GRILLED MUSHROOMS WITH PESTO SAUCE

This is one of the fastest dishes I know. It makes an excellent starter for four or eight people (depending on the rest of the menu) or you can serve the mushrooms with one of the rice dishes in Chapter 12 as a main course for two.

8 large flat mushrooms
120g pesto sauce
freshly ground black pepper

1. Preheat the grill to medium-hot. Spread 1 tablespoon of the pesto over the gills of each mushroom. Season with pepper.

2. Place under the grill and cook for 5–6 minutes, depending on the thickness of the mushrooms and how well done you like them. Serve hot.

GRILLED TOFU
WITH BALSAMIC VINEGAR (V)

The longer you can leave the raisins to plump up in the balsamic vinegar mixture the better the flavour will be. Serve with vegetable kebabs and rice.

3 tbsp raisins
1 tbsp lemon juice
1 tsp balsamic vinegar
225g firm tofu
mixed salad leaves, including well-flavoured leaves such as
  watercress, rocket or baby spinach
2 tbsp pine nuts, toasted
extra virgin olive oil to serve

1. Put the raisins in a bowl with the lemon juice and balsamic vinegar and leave to stand.
2. Preheat the grill to hot. Cut the tofu into four thick slices and place under the grill. Cook for about 1–2 minutes on each side until the tofu is golden.
3. Arrange the salad leaves on four plates and place the grilled tofu on top. Spoon the raisins and their juices over the tofu and sprinkle with the toasted pine nuts. Drizzle with olive oil and serve at once.

GRILLED MUSHROOMS
WITH YELLOW TOMATO SALSA (V)

I love the spicy flavour of Mexican salsa. I have never come across it served with mushrooms in any Mexican cookbook, but it really works very well.

8 large flat mushrooms
extra virgin olive oil for brushing
salt and freshly ground black pepper
1–2 garlic cloves, crushed (optional)

Yellow tomato salsa
450g yellow tomatoes, skinned, seeded and chopped
1 tbsp grated lime zest
juice of 1 lime
1 bunch of spring onions, chopped
6 tbsp chopped fresh coriander
1 green chilli, seeded and chopped

1. Start by making the salsa. Mix all the ingredients together in a bowl and leave to stand in the fridge.
2. Preheat the grill to hot. Brush the mushrooms all over with oil and sprinkle with salt, pepper and garlic, if using. Place under the grill and cook for 4–5 minutes, depending on the thickness of the mushrooms. Brush with more oil if required.
3. When the mushrooms are cooked through, spoon a little of the salsa onto each one and return to the grill for a couple of minutes. Serve hot.

GRILLED FETA CHEESE WITH OLIVES

A Greek restaurant in Camden Town was the inspiration for this dish. The rain was streaming down the windows, the temperature was way below anything you might experience in Greece and I wanted something hot. Grilled cheese with olives was the answer and a large glass of ouzo!

225g feta cheese
6 tbsp extra virgin olive oil
2 pitta breads, split open to make two thin slices
grated zest and juice of 1 lemon
freshly ground black pepper
a pinch of dried thyme
24 black olives, stoned and halved

1. Cut the cheese into slices (don't worry if they are rather crumbly) and brush with a little of the olive oil. Preheat the grill to medium.
2. Toast the pitta bread lightly on both sides and top with the cheese slices. Place under the grill and cook for a couple of minutes. Transfer to serving plates.
3. In a saucepan, gently heat the remaining olive oil with the lemon zest and juice, thyme and black pepper. Don't let it get too hot.
4. Sprinkle the olives over the cheese toasts and spoon on the lemon-flavoured olive oil. Serve at once.

STUFFED MARROW RINGS WITH AUBERGINES AND TOMATOES (V)

This method of cooking marrow is very quick and you do not need to use the oven. However, you will need to keep your eye on the marrow while it is cooking as it can easily overcook and go soggy. I like to catch it when it still has a slight bite to it.

1 vegetable marrow (about 1kg)
salt
extra virgin olive oil for brushing
1 large aubergine
2 large tomatoes, skinned and sliced
Stuffing
2 tbsp extra virgin olive oil
2 onions, peeled and finely chopped
2 large carrots, peeled and grated
100ml vegetable stock
100g pine nuts, toasted
4–6 black olives, stoned and chopped
2–3 large sprigs of basil, chopped
salt and freshly ground black pepper

1. Cut the marrow into eight thick slices. Scoop the seeds out of the centre. Plunge the marrow rings into salted boiling water and cook for about 10 minutes until just tender. Drain and dry on kitchen paper.

2. While the marrow is cooking, preheat the grill and brush a baking sheet lightly with oil. Trim the ends off the aubergine and cut into eight thick slices. Brush with oil, place on the baking sheet and place under a hot grill for 3–4 minutes until lightly browned. Turn the slices over, brush with oil and grill for another 3–4 minutes.

3. To make the stuffing, heat the oil in a saucepan and fry the onions until lightly browned. Add the carrots and stock and cook, stirring from time to time, for about 5–6 minutes until the carrots are softened. Then add all the remaining stuffing ingredients, season to taste and mix well.

4. Place one ring of marrow on each slice of grilled aubergine. Fill the cavities in the marrow with the stuffing mixture and top with a slice of tomato.

5. Drizzle with more olive oil and put the baking sheet back under the grill for 3–4 minutes. Serve at once.

BANANA KEBABS (V)

Sorrel is occasionally seen in supermarkets and its tangy flavour goes very well with bananas. If I can't find sorrel I sometimes use basil or rocket but the flavour is rather different.

8 baby sweetcorn
12 sorrel leaves
3 large bananas, peeled and each cut into 4 large chunks
12 cherry tomatoes
salt and freshly ground black pepper

1. Preheat the grill or barbecue. Put the baby corn in a saucepan of boiling water and cook for 10 minutes. Drain.
2. Plunge the sorrel leaves into boiling water and remove immediately; plunge them into cold water, then drain on kitchen paper.
3. Wrap the blanched sorrel leaves around the banana pieces, covering as much of the banana as possible, and thread onto skewers with the corn and cherry tomatoes. Season with salt and pepper.
4. Place under the grill or on the barbecue and cook for about 6–8 minutes, turning frequently. Serve at once.

ONION AND MUSHROOM KEBABS (V)

If I can find them, I use roasted baby onions packed in olive oil for a really speedy version of this recipe.

225g small pickling onions
225g large button mushrooms
150ml dry white wine
1 tbsp tomato purée
1 bay leaf
½ tsp fennel or celery seeds
1 large red pepper, seeded and cut into quarters
2 tbsp extra virgin olive oil
salt and freshly ground black pepper

1. Preheat the grill or barbecue. Put the onions, mushrooms, wine, tomato purée, bay leaf and fennel or celery seeds in a saucepan and bring to the boil. Cover with a lid and simmer for 5–8 minutes until the onions have softened.
2. Grill the pepper quarters for a minute or two but do not char. Cut into smaller pieces.
3. Thread the onions, mushrooms and peppers onto skewers, brush with olive oil and season with salt and pepper.
4. Place under the grill or on the barbecue and cook for 5–6 minutes until lightly charred, turning from time to time. Serve hot.

TOFU AND FENNEL KEBABS

Tofu should not be overcooked, so make sure that the fennel is cooked to your liking before threading onto the kebab.

16 bay leaves
3 tbsp natural yogurt
1 tbsp lemon juice
1 garlic clove, peeled and crushed
250g firm tofu, cut into 8 squares
3 small to medium bulbs of fennel, trimmed and cut into quarters
75ml dry white wine
2 tbsp extra virgin olive oil
salt and freshly ground black pepper

1. Soak the bay leaves in water so that they will not burn when grilled.
2. Mix the yogurt with the lemon juice and garlic in a bowl or shallow dish, add the tofu and leave to marinate.
3. Put the fennel in a saucepan with the wine. Bring to the boil and simmer for 10–12 minutes until almost tender. Drain and dry on kitchen paper, keeping the cooking liquor for stock or soup.
4. Preheat the grill. Thread the fennel on to four skewers with the squares of tofu and bay leaves, placing the bay leaves on either side of every piece of tofu. Brush with olive oil and season with salt and pepper.
5. Grill the kebabs for 2–3 minutes, turning them from time to time so that the tofu browns evenly. Serve at once.

VARIATION

Halloumi cheese would work well in place of the tofu – but check that it is suitable for vegetarians.

GRILLED SWEETCORN
WITH SPICY HERB BUTTER

It is a good idea to boil corn cobs for a short time before placing under the grill or on the barbecue. This stops the kernels from drying out. However, if the corn is very fresh indeed this step can be omitted.

The spicy butter can be made up to four days in advance. You could also serve it on baked potatoes.

4 sweetcorn cobs, with the sheaths removed

Spicy herb butter
125g salted butter, softened
1 tbsp chopped fresh coriander
1 tsp dried mixed herbs
1 tsp ground coriander
salt and freshly ground black pepper

1. Preheat the grill or barbecue.
2. To make the spicy herb butter, mix all the ingredients together, seasoning to taste. Roll into a log shape, wrap in butter paper (or greaseproof) and place in the fridge to set for at least 15 minutes.
3. Cook the corn in salted boiling water for about 6–7 minutes. Drain and dry on kitchen paper.
4. Place the corn on the barbecue or under the grill for about 5 minutes, turning occasionally, until lightly browned. Slice the spicy herb butter into rounds and serve with the corn.

GRILLED VEGETABLES IN A BUN

This is a vegetarian take on the hamburger. It is very versatile: you can use different vegetables, such as sliced courgettes, quartered peppers or large flat mushrooms in place of the aubergines.

1 aubergine, cut into 4 thick slices
extra virgin olive oil for brushing
1 beef tomato, cut into 4 thick slices
200g feta cheese, cut into 4 slices
4 sesame buns, sliced open
salt and freshly ground black pepper
2 tbsp tomato ketchup

1. Preheat the grill or barbecue. Brush the aubergine slices on both sides with olive oil and grill for 3–4 minutes until lightly browned on one side.
2. Turn the aubergine slices and add the tomato and feta slices to the grill. Grill the aubergine for a further 3–4 minutes on the other side until lightly browned and cooked through. Turn the tomato and feta after 1–2 minutes to cook on both sides.
3. Toast the buns on the grill until lightly seared. Place an aubergine slice on the base of each bun and top with a slice of tomato and feta. Season and top with ketchup and the top of the bun. Serve at once.

VARIATIONS
Serve with mayonnaise or pesto sauce in place of the tomato ketchup or add one of the salsas from elsewhere in the book (see pages 103, 104 and 150)

MUSHROOM, CARROT AND TOFU BURGERS WITH FRESH CORIANDER (V)

Vegetable burgers taste much better if they are crisp on the outside and really moist on the inside. To achieve this I always use plenty of fresh vegetables in the mix. Make sure they are grated or chopped finely for even cooking.

175g carrots, peeled and grated
125g mushrooms, wiped and very finely chopped
1 onion, peeled and very finely chopped
1 garlic clove, peeled and crushed
225g firm tofu
125g fresh wholemeal breadcrumbs
25g chopped fresh coriander
25g chopped fresh parsley
salt and freshly ground black pepper
extra virgin olive oil for brushing
8 small sesame buns to serve

Sauce
2 tbsp tahini (sesame seed paste)
2 tbsp soya yogurt (or natural yogurt)
juice of 1 lemon
1 tsp sesame oil

1. Put the prepared vegetables and garlic in a bowl and mix well together.
2. Mash the tofu with a fork and add to the vegetables, together with the breadcrumbs and herbs. Mix well together and season to taste.
3. Preheat the grill. Shape the vegetable mixture into eight small burgers and brush with oil. Grill for 5 minutes on each side, brushing with a little oil from time to time.
4. To make the sauce, mix all the ingredients together, adding a little water if the mixture is too thick. Serve with the burgers in warm sesame buns.

LENTIL BURGERS (V)

My father was an excellent cook and this is one of his specialities. The burgers are crisp on the outside and light and soft in the centre. He was rather vague about the quantities he used, but a couple of testing sessions solved the problem. Serve in burger buns, with salad, or with African Red Beans (see page 244).

125g red or yellow split lentils
225g button mushrooms, chopped
300ml vegetable stock
a pinch of dried mixed herbs
salt and freshly ground black pepper
3 tbsp millet or oat flakes
2 tbsp extra virgin olive oil

1. Put the lentils, mushrooms, stock, herbs, salt and pepper in a saucepan and bring to the boil. Cover with a lid and cook over a fairly high heat for 20 minutes.
2. Mash the contents of the pan with a potato masher and then shape into eight balls. Flatten into burgers and coat with the millet or oat flakes.
3. Preheat the grill or barbecue. Brush the burgers with oil and place on a piece of foil. Cook on the barbecue or under the grill for 3–4 minutes on each side. Serve hot.

CHAPTER 9
STIR-FRIES AND WOK COOKERY

Stir-frying is a very quick method of cooking. Make sure that the oil is hot before adding the ingredients. A non-stick wok is useful for some dishes but not essential. If you do not have a wok you can use a deep-sided frying pan, preferably with rounded sides. However, you will need to take more care to keep the food on the move and to make sure that none of it sticks in the corners. If the ingredients seem too dry or are starting to burn during cooking, add a tablespoon of stock, wine or water and continue stir-frying over a medium to high heat.

The length of time you need to stir-fry vegetables depends on how crisp you like them to be. Put root vegetables and other ingredients that require longer cooking into the wok first, adding more tender vegetables such as asparagus, mangetout and green vegetables later. Bean sprouts do not take long to cook at all, so add at the last minute.

All recipes are for four people.

HOT SPICED CABBAGE (V)

The toasted spices and orange juice give a wonderfully aromatic flavour to this cabbage dish. Serve with rice and curries.

2 tbsp raisins
50ml orange juice
a little grated orange zest
2 tbsp cider vinegar
3 tbsp extra virgin olive oil
1 tsp cumin seeds
1 tsp black or yellow mustard seeds
1 onion, peeled and sliced
175g green cabbage, very finely shredded
75g red cabbage, very finely shredded

Garnish
2 tbsp flaked almonds, toasted

1. Put the raisins in a cup with the orange juice and zest and the vinegar.
2. Heat the oil in a non-stick wok or deep frying pan. Fry the cumin seeds and mustard seeds for about 1 minute until they begin to pop. Add the onion and cabbage and stir-fry over a medium heat for 3–4 minutes.
3. Pour in the raisins and orange juice and zest and cook for a further 1–2 minutes. Serve hot from the pan, garnished with toasted flaked almonds.

STIR-FRIED COURGETTES
WITH GARLIC AND OLIVES (V)

These flavours are closer to Mediterranean cuisine than Chinese but the combination works very well as a stir-fry, served with simple egg noodles.

2 tbsp extra virgin olive oil
2 shallots or 4–6 spring onions, finely chopped
2–3 large garlic cloves, peeled and sliced
450g courgettes, cut into large dice
16–20 black olives, stoned and chopped
salt and freshly ground black pepper
4–5 tbsp vegetable stock
1 tbsp dry sherry

1. Heat the oil in a non-stick wok or deep frying pan, add the shallots or spring onions and the garlic and stir-fry for a minute or so over a high heat.
2. Add the courgettes and stir-fry for 2–3 minutes. Add all the remaining ingredients and bring to the boil. Cook over a high heat for 1 minute, then serve at once.

STIR-FRIED ASPARAGUS AND MANGETOUT WITH LEMON (V)

The lemony flavours of lemongrass, tamarind paste and lemons themselves are widely used in oriental cooking and I have been experimenting in matching them to different vegetables. This recipe uses fresh lemons to give a very clean flavour to a stir-fry dish in the Chinese style. However, you could replace the lemon with tamarind paste and add a teaspoonful of honey and some chilli pepper to give a Thai feel to the dish. I prefer to leave the cooking liquid quite runny, but if you like you can thicken it with a little cornflour.

2 tbsp extra virgin olive oil
1 lemon, very finely sliced
1 garlic clove, peeled and crushed
350g frozen asparagus
175g mangetout, trimmed
juice of 1 lemon
3 tbsp vegetable stock
1 tbsp light soy sauce
salt and freshly ground black pepper
a little cornflour mixed with 1 tbsp water (optional)

1. Heat the oil in a wok or deep frying pan. Add the lemon slices carefully – they may spit when they hit the fat – and stir-fry for a couple of minutes.
2. Using a slotted spoon, remove all the lemon slices from the pan and reserve about half of the thinnest; discard the rest.
3. Return the pan to the heat, add the garlic, stir, then add the asparagus and mangetout. Stir-fry for 2 minutes, then add the lemon juice, stock, soy sauce, salt and pepper. Bring the mixture to the boil and cook over a high heat for a further 2–3 minutes. If liked, stir in the cornflour to thicken the liquid. Serve at once, with the reserved lemon slices.

EASTERN LEAVES WITH LEMONGRASS AND CORIANDER (V)

The inspiration for this recipe comes from Thai cooking. It has a spicy, sweet and sour quality which is quite unusual with greens. Serve it as part of a medley of Asian dishes, such as Singapore Noodles (see page 137) and Curried Chestnuts (see page 210).

2 tbsp extra virgin olive oil
3 pieces of lemongrass, cut into lengths
2 garlic cloves, peeled and sliced
small head of Chinese leaves, sliced
400g Chinese greens such as bok choy, torn into large pieces
4 tbsp dry white wine
1 tsp light soy sauce
salt and freshly ground black pepper
1 tsp sugar
½ tsp cayenne or chilli pepper
small bunch of coriander, chopped

1. Heat the oil in a non-stick wok or deep frying pan and stir-fry the lemongrass and garlic for a minute or so.
2. Add the Chinese leaves and stir-fry for 2 minutes. Add all the remaining ingredients except the coriander and bring to the boil. Cook for 1 minute, then add the coriander. Cook for a further minute, then serve at once.

TOFU WITH MUSHROOMS (V)

Depending on the brand of chilli bean sauce that you use, this can be quite a spicy dish. I usually choose a Sichuan black bean sauce which is pretty hot. Serve with rice.

extra virgin olive oil or groundnut oil for deep-frying (about 450ml), plus 1 tbsp
450g firm tofu, cubed
1½ tbsp finely chopped garlic
2 tsp finely chopped fresh root ginger
50g spring onions, coarsely chopped
100g button mushrooms, halved or quartered, depending on size
2 tsp chilli bean sauce
1½ tbsp dry sherry
1 tbsp soy sauce
1 tsp salt
½ tsp freshly ground black pepper
2 tbsp vegetable stock or water

1. Heat the oil in a deep-fat fryer or large wok until it is very hot but not smoking. Deep-fry the tofu in batches until lightly browned. Drain on kitchen paper.
2. Heat a wok or deep frying pan until very hot. Add 1 tablespoon of oil then add the garlic, ginger and spring onions. Stir-fry for a few seconds, then add the mushrooms. Stir-fry for 30 seconds, then add all the remaining ingredients.
3. Reduce the heat to very low, add the tofu, cover with a lid and simmer for 8 minutes. Serve hot.

DICED TOFU WITH PEAS (V)

This is a colourful mixture to serve with fried noodles or plain bulgur wheat. Add the tofu at the very last minute and take care not to overcook it.

2 tbsp extra virgin olive oil
1 garlic clove, peeled and crushed
1 bunch of spring onions, coarsely chopped
1 small red pepper, seeded and finely diced
50g frozen sweetcorn
175g frozen peas
1 tbsp dry sherry
3 tbsp vegetable stock
a pinch of five-spice powder
salt and freshly ground black pepper
2 tbsp chopped fresh parsley
1 tbsp chopped fresh basil
175g firm tofu, finely diced

1. Heat the oil in a wok or deep frying pan and stir-fry the garlic and spring onions for 1 minute.
2. Add the red pepper and stir-fry for 2 minutes. Add the frozen vegetables and toss the contents of the pan well together.
3. Add the sherry and stock, five-spice powder, salt and pepper and turn up the heat. Cook for 2–3 minutes, stirring all the time.
4. Add the herbs and tofu and toss over a high heat for about 30 seconds or so until heated through. Serve at once.

SAUTÉED SPINACH WITH GINGER AND HAZELNUTS (V)

Spinach cooks very quickly so take care not to overcook. Serve this on a bed of stir-fried noodles with grilled feta cheese or tofu.

1 tbsp extra virgin olive oil
2cm fresh root ginger, peeled and cut into thin strips
50g hazelnuts, coarsely chopped
4 spring onions, finely chopped
1kg young spinach leaves
2 tbsp Chinese soup stock (see page 12)

1. Heat the oil in a wok or deep frying pan over a high heat. Add the ginger, hazelnuts and spring onions and stir-fry for 1 minute.
2. Add the spinach and stock and toss with the other ingredients for 2–3 minutes until the leaves wilt. Serve at once.

ORANGE STIR-FRY VEGETABLES
WITH TOFU (V)

Orange goes extremely well with the cauliflower and the leeks in this dish and the tofu takes up all the flavours. Serve with Chinese egg noodles, boiled rice, couscous or bulgur.

grated zest and juice of 2 oranges
225g firm tofu, diced
2 tbsp tahini (sesame seed paste)
4 tbsp vegetable stock
2 tbsp light soy sauce
2 tbsp extra virgin olive oil
2.5cm fresh root ginger, peeled and cut into thin sticks
1 bunch of spring onions, cut on the slant
1 small cauliflower, cut into florets
1 red pepper, seeded and sliced
2 large leeks, trimmed and sliced thinly
salt and freshly ground black pepper

1. Sprinkle the orange zest over the tofu and keep on one side.
2. Spoon the tahini into a cup and gradually stir in the stock and then the soy sauce. Keep on one side with the orange juice.
3. Heat 1 tablespoon of the oil in a wok or deep frying pan over a high heat and stir-fry the ginger and spring onions for 1 minute. Add the cauliflower and red pepper and stir-fry for 2–3 minutes. Add the leeks and cook for another minute or so.
4. Pour in the orange juice and bring to the boil. Simmer for a minute or two until the vegetables are cooked to your liking. Add the tofu and orange zest and toss together until the tofu is heated through.
5. Finally, add the tahini mixture and stir over a medium heat until the sauce thickens. This will happen quite quickly. Spoon the tofu and vegetables over your chosen accompaniment, season and serve at once.

STIR-FRIED TOFU AND GARLIC IN FIELD MUSHROOMS (V)

This recipe is sometimes made with shallots, but as a garlic fan, I decided to use this pungent vegetable instead. It gives a well-flavoured stir-fry base, which is important if there's no time to marinate the tofu. Serve with boiled rice.

4 very large field mushrooms or 8 smaller ones
4 tbsp groundnut oil
salt and freshly ground black pepper
1 tbsp roasted sesame oil mixed with 1 tbsp groundnut oil
4 whole garlic cloves, peeled and sliced
1 tbsp grated fresh root ginger
1 bunch of spring onions, cut into 2.5cm lengths
1 tsp grated orange zest
4 tbsp soy sauce
225g firm tofu, cut into cubes

1. Preheat the grill to medium. Trim the mushroom stalks. Season and brush the mushrooms with groundnut oil and grill on both sides for about 5 minutes until the mushrooms are beginning to soften.
2. Heat the sesame oil in a non-stick wok or deep frying pan over a medium–high heat and stir-fry the garlic for about 1 minute until softened.
3. Add the ginger and spring onions and stir-fry for about 30 seconds.
4. Add the orange zest, soy sauce and tofu cubes and toss over a high heat until well mixed. Spoon over the grilled mushrooms and serve at once.

CHOP SUEY (V)

Chop suey is not a traditional Chinese dish: it was devised by Chinese labourers working on the Californian railways in the mid-nineteenth century. Chop suey meant 'anything that is to hand'. So it is a very useful dish for using up whatever is left in the salad or vegetable box – all you really need is bean sprouts.

2 tbsp extra virgin olive oil
250g mixed vegetables, cut into strips
4 tbsp Chinese soup stock (see page 12)
175g bean sprouts
soy sauce
a little cornflour mixed with 1 tbsp water (optional)

1. Heat the oil in a wok or deep frying pan and stir-fry the vegetables for 1–2 minutes. Add the stock and continue to cook until the vegetables are al dente or just firm to the bite.
2. Add the bean sprouts and a little soy sauce and toss well together. If you like, stir in the cornflour to thicken the sauce.

SUGGESTIONS FOR VEGETABLE COMBINATIONS

- Red and green peppers with spring onions and mangetout
- Broccoli with carrots and onions
- Red onions with celeriac sticks and ginger

STIR-FRIED EGGS WITH BROCCOLI

Stir-fried eggs are rather like scrambled eggs, but they should not be too broken up. The method is used both in China and in Italy. In the former they are served with egg noodles and in the latter with pasta – take your pick.

150ml vegetable stock
450g broccoli, cut into pieces
2 tbsp extra virgin oil
¼ small green pepper, seeded and diced
¼ small red pepper, seeded and diced
2 tbsp finely chopped spring onions
4 eggs, beaten
2 tbsp water
salt and freshly ground black pepper

1. Bring the stock to the boil in a saucepan, add the broccoli and boil for 3–4 minutes until just tender. Drain and keep warm.
2. Heat the oil in a non-stick wok or deep frying pan and fry the peppers and spring onions for 2 minutes.
3. Mix the eggs, water, salt and pepper and pour over the vegetables. Stir-fry for about 1–2 minutes. As the eggs begin to set, add the broccoli, stir and serve at once.

STIR-FRIED EGGS WITH BROAD BEANS AND PEPPERS

East meets West in this dish, which is fresh and crunchy as well as being quite creamy.

4 eggs, beaten
1 tbsp milk
2 tbsp chopped fresh parsley
salt and freshly ground black pepper
knob of butter
1 tbsp extra virgin olive oil
2 leeks, trimmed and finely sliced
1 red pepper, seeded and chopped
350g fresh or thawed frozen broad beans
1 tbsp soy sauce
2 tbsp vegetable stock
1 tbsp dry sherry

1. Mix the eggs with the milk, parsley, salt and pepper.
2. Heat the butter in a non-stick wok or deep frying pan and add the eggs. Stir-fry the eggs so that they do not set into a solid mass but not so vigorously as to scramble them. When the eggs are just set, transfer to a plate and keep warm.
3. Wipe out the wok with kitchen paper and put back over a high heat. Add the oil and stir-fry the leeks, red pepper and beans for 2–3 minutes.
4. Add the soy sauce, stock and sherry and continue to stir-fry over a high heat until the liquid has almost evaporated and the beans are cooked through. Return the eggs to the pan, toss well and serve at once.

BRAISED SPICY AUBERGINES (V)

The Chinese use their woks to braise food as well as to stir-fry it.
The results can be quite rich and spicy. Serve with rice or noodles.

2 tbsp extra virgin olive oil
2 tbsp finely chopped garlic
1½ tbsp finely chopped fresh root ginger
2 tbsp finely chopped spring onions, white part only
450g small, thin aubergines, sliced
2 tbsp dark soy sauce
1 tbsp chilli bean sauce
1 tbsp yellow bean sauce
1 tbsp sugar
1 tbsp Chinese black vinegar or cider vinegar
2 tsp Sichuan peppercorns, roasted and ground
300ml vegetable stock or water
2 tbsp chopped spring onions, green tops only, to garnish

1. Heat a non-stick wok or deep frying pan until it is very hot.
   Add the oil and when it is really hot add the garlic, ginger
   and spring onions and stir-fry for 30 seconds. Add the
   aubergines and stir-fry for a further minute.
2. Add all the remaining ingredients (except the spring onion
   tops), reduce the heat and simmer, uncovered, for 10–15
   minutes until the aubergines are tender. Increase the heat
   and stir until the liquid has thickened. Serve hot, sprinkled
   with green spring onion tops.

BRAISED GEM LETTUCES

Gem lettuces remain reasonably firm when cooked in sauce and so work well in this Chinese braising recipe. You could also try this with radicchio or chicory (Belgian endive).

grated zest and juice of 1 orange
2 tbsp soy sauce
1 tbsp dry sherry
1 tsp grated fresh root ginger
½ tsp five-spice powder
1 tbsp raisins
4 Little Gem lettuces, cut into quarters

1. Put the orange zest and juice, soy sauce and sherry into a wok and add the ginger, five-spice powder and raisins. Bring to the boil and cook for 1 minute.
2. Add the lettuces and cook over a high heat for about 2–3 minutes. The lettuces should heat through and soften a little but they should not be limp. Serve at once.

GLAZED GARLIC TOFU (V)

This makes a well-flavoured tofu to serve with almost any of the rice dishes in Chapter 12. I sometimes add Chinese five-spice powder or toasted sesame seeds and fresh coriander and serve with plain boiled rice or fried noodles.

1 head of garlic, cloves separated and peeled
½ tsp dried chilli flakes
3 tbsp soy sauce
150ml cider vinegar
3 tbsp clear honey
225g firm tofu

1. Blend the garlic, chilli flakes, soy sauce, vinegar and honey in a food processor or blender. Transfer to a wok or deep frying pan and cook over a high heat, stirring from time to time, until reduced by about half.
2. Cut the tofu into thick strips or large cubes. Add to the garlic and vinegar mixture and poach for about 4 minutes until the tofu is heated through. Serve hot.

CHAPTER 10
PIES AND BAKES

Filo pastry is the only kind of pastry that will cook within half an hour if you are also preparing the filling in that time. It also has the advantage of being ready rolled. It is very easy to use: the secret is not to be shy of using oil to moisten the dough. To get the best result each sheet of filo must be brushed liberally with olive oil before being cooked.

Packs of filo pastry come in various sizes, so you may need to cut the sheets to the dimensions given in the recipes. Some recipes suggest using two layers of pastry instead of three as this will be faster to cook – but the end result may not be as crispy.

As well as filo pies I have included a number of baked vegetable dishes and a couple of recipes for baked eggs. Eggs cook very quickly in the oven. The simplest method is to cook them *en cocotte* (baked in a ramekin) with cream or a melted soft cheese such as Boursin.

All recipes are for four people unless otherwise stated.

PRUNE AND CHEESE PURSES

These parcels make a wonderful starter or a light meal. They may seem a little fiddly to prepare but it can be done in about 10–15 minutes while the oven is heating up. They then take about 10–12 minutes to cook – just time to prepare a green salad to serve with them.

Makes 8 parcels

3–4 tbsp extra virgin olive oil
75g blue cheese
50g curd cheese
8 large ready-to-eat prunes, stoned and halved
8 walnut halves
6–8 sheets of filo pastry

1. Preheat the oven to 200°C/Gas 6. Brush a baking sheet with oil.
2. Mash the two cheeses together with a fork and use the mixture to sandwich the prune halves together, adding a walnut half in the centre.
3. Cut the filo pastry into 16 x15cm squares. Brush two pastry squares with olive oil and place one on top of the other.
4. Place a prune 'sandwich' in the centre. Gather up the edges of the pastry over the prunes and twist lightly to seal. Place on the baking sheet. Repeat this process to make 8 parcels.
5. Bake for 10–12 minutes until crisp and golden. Serve hot.

FRUITY CHEESE PARCELS

You can use any kind of soft rind cheese for these crispy filo pastry parcels, but a log-shaped goat's cheese works well. Add your favourite fruit chutney – the spicier the better. Serve with stir-fried mangetout to make an elegant main course.

Makes 8 parcels

3–4 tbsp extra virgin olive oil
1 small (approx. 120g) log-shaped goat's cheese
6–8 sheets of filo pastry
8 tsp curried fruit chutney

1. Preheat the oven to 200°C/Gas 6. Brush a baking sheet with oil. Cut the cheese into eight equal slices.
2. Cut the filo pastry into 16 x 15cm squares. Brush two pastry squares with olive oil and place one on top of the other.
3. Place a piece of cheese in the centre of each square and top with a teaspoonful of chutney. Gather up the edges of the pastry over the cheese and pinch together. Place on the baking sheet. Repeat this process to make 8 parcels.
4. Bake for 10–12 minutes until crisp and golden. Serve hot.

VARIATIONS

If you do not have any chutney to hand, sprinkle the goat's cheese with a mixture of ground nutmeg and dried thyme or with freshly chopped mint or parsley.

SPINACH AND CHESTNUT FILO PIE

This unusual filling is based on a southern Italian recipe for a filling for pasta. I use a canned purée made with roasted chestnuts, which have a particularly good flavour, but any unsweetened chestnut purée will do. I usually use cream cheese, but if you prefer a lower fat content or want to avoid dairy food, silken tofu also works very well. This will serve four to six people, depending on the rest of the menu.

4 tbsp extra virgin olive oil
6 sheets of filo pastry, cut to 27 x 17cm

Filling
450g fresh spinach
250g cream cheese, curd cheese, ricotta or silken tofu
200g canned or vacuum-packed unsweetened chestnut purée
grated zest and juice of ½ lemon
1 tsp dried thyme or oregano
1 tsp coriander seeds, crushed
salt and freshly ground black pepper

1. Preheat the oven to 200°C/Gas 6. Brush a 27 x 17cm Swiss roll tin with oil.
2. To make the filling, steam the spinach until it begins to wilt. Drain well and keep on one side.
3. Mix the cheese or tofu with the chestnut purée, lemon zest and juice, thyme or oregano, coriander, salt and pepper until smooth.
4. Line the Swiss roll tin with three layers of filo pastry, brushing each layer with oil as you go. Spoon on the chestnut mixture

and then spread the spinach over the top. Cover with three more layers of oil-brushed filo. Cut into four or six pieces, using a sharp knife.

5. Bake for 15 minutes until crisp and golden. Serve hot.

VARIATIONS

For a subtle oriental flavour substitute 2–3 tablespoons soy sauce for the lemon juice and add a pinch of five-spice powder.

If you are in a hurry you could use just four sheets of filo (two layers on the bottom, two on top); the pie should then be ready in about 12–13 minutes.

CELERIAC AND RICOTTA FILO PIE

Celeriac has a delicate flavour, somewhere between celery and parsnips. In America and elsewhere the vegetable is known as celery root. You need to buy a large celeriac to get a reasonable amount of flesh as it usually needs quite a lot of trimming.

This pie will serve four to six people, partly depending on your choice of accompaniments. The mixture can also be used to make individual pies (see page 184). Or if you are in a hurry you could use just four sheets of filo (two layers on the bottom, two on top); the pie should then be ready in about 12–13 minutes, but it will not be as crispy.

4 tbsp extra virgin olive oil
6 sheets of filo pastry, cut to 27 x 17cm

Filling
500g celeriac, trimmed, peeled and coarsely grated
4 tbsp dry white wine or vegetable stock
225g ricotta cheese
40g sun-dried tomatoes, chopped
4 tbsp chopped fresh parsley
salt and freshly ground black pepper

1. Preheat the oven to 200°C/Gas 6. Brush a 27 x17 cm Swiss roll tin with oil.

2. To make the filling, cook the celeriac in the wine or stock for about 5–6 minutes. Allow the liquid to boil fast and stir very frequently until the celeriac starts to soften.

3. Mix the ricotta and sun-dried tomatoes in a bowl and add the cooked celeriac, parsley, salt and pepper.

4. Line the Swiss roll tin with three layers of filo pastry, brushing each layer with oil as you go. Spoon on the celeriac mixture and spread flat with a knife. Cover with three more layers of oil-brushed filo. Cut into four or six pieces, using a sharp knife.

5. Bake for 15 minutes until crisp and golden. Serve hot.

TOFU AND TOMATO PLATTER PIES

Filo pastry pies look very attractive when cooked in individual dishes. I use dishes with a base diameter of 10cm and sloping sides, with a rim diameter of 14cm. If you do not have any suitable dishes, the mixture can be cooked in a Swiss roll tin (see pages 180–1). Either way, if you are in a hurry you could use just two layers of pastry on the bottom, two on top; the pies should then be ready in about 12–13 minutes but will not be as crispy.

4 tbsp extra virgin olive oil
8–12 sheets of filo pastry

Filling
2 tbsp extra virgin olive oil
1 garlic clove, peeled and chopped
2 onions, peeled and chopped
4 tomatoes, skinned, seeded and chopped
285g firm tofu
3 tbsp coarsely torn basil leaves
2 tbsp tomato purée
salt and freshly ground black pepper

1. Preheat the oven to 200°C/Gas 6. Grease four individual pie dishes with olive oil.
2. To make the filling, heat the oil in a small frying pan and fry the garlic and onions for about 5 minutes until lightly browned. Stir in the tomatoes and cook for another 2 minutes.
3. Put the tofu in a large bowl and mash with a fork. Add the contents of the frying pan and the basil, tomato purée, salt and pepper. Mix well.

4. Cut the filo pastry into 24 x 15cm squares. Line each pie dish with three layers of filo pastry, brushing each layer with oil as you go. Spoon on the tofu and tomato mixture and level with a knife. Cover with three more layers of oil-brushed filo.

5. Place on a baking sheet and bake for 15 minutes. Serve hot.

MEDITERRANEAN VEGETABLE AND FETA TART

This is a colourful open tart which can be served as a main course. Alternatively you could cut it into smaller pieces to serve as finger food at a party. Vegans can use tofu in place of feta.

extra virgin olive oil for brushing
1 red pepper, seeded and cut into quarters
2 small courgettes, sliced lengthways
4 sheets of filo pastry, cut to 27 x 17cm
2 tomatoes, sliced
225g feta cheese, crumbled
salt and freshly ground black pepper

1. Preheat the oven to 200°C/Gas 6. Brush a 27 x 17cm Swiss roll tin with oil.

2. Steam the red pepper and courgettes for 10 minutes until softened.

3. Line the Swiss roll tin with four layers of filo pastry, brushing each layer with oil as you go.

4. Arrange the steamed vegetables and tomatoes in rows or in a pattern on the pastry. Sprinkle with the feta cheese, salt and pepper and drizzle with more olive oil.

5. Bake for about 10–12 minutes. Cut into squares to serve.

BAKED EGGS WITH TARRAGON CREAM

Use small ramekin dishes for these baked eggs. You can ring the changes by using different herbs: try chives or chervil.

100ml double cream
50g soft cheese
2 tbsp finely chopped fresh tarragon or 2 tsp dried tarragon
salt and freshly ground black pepper
4 eggs

1. Preheat the oven to 180°C/Gas 4.
2. Put the cream in a small saucepan and carefully stir in the soft cheese. Heat to just below the boil, then stir in the tarragon, salt and pepper.
3. Break the eggs into four ramekin dishes and spoon the hot cream mixture on top. Bake for about 12–15 minutes, depending on how runny you like the yolks, and serve at once.

VARIATION

It is even quicker to use crème fraîche in place of the cream and soft cheese mixture – no need to heat the crème fraîche. Simply place a tablespoonful in the base of each ramekin, add the eggs and top with another spoonful of crème fraîche.

HORSERADISH CARROTS WITH EGGS

This simple combination of ingredients gives a wonderfully delicate balance of flavours.

2 tbsp extra virgin olive oil, plus extra for greasing
350g carrots, peeled and coarsely grated
1 small onion, peeled and grated
1 tbsp creamed horseradish
salt and freshly ground black pepper
4 eggs

1. Preheat the oven to 200°C/Gas 6. Grease four ramekin dishes.
2. Heat a frying pan or wok over a medium heat, add the oil and stir-fry the carrots and onion for 3–4 minutes until they start to soften. Add the horseradish and stir to mix thoroughly, season to taste with salt and pepper and transfer to the ramekins.
3. Break an egg on top of each ramekin and bake for 10–15 minutes until the eggs are cooked to your liking.

VARIATION

Use thawed frozen spinach and a small crushed garlic clove in place of the carrots, and double cream instead of horseradish.

EGG AND VEGETABLE NESTS

There are many variations on this theme; the recipe here is the most colourful version. If you do not have time to cook the eggs in the oven they can be cooked on the top of the stove. Simply break the eggs into the vegetables in the frying pan and cover with a lid; they will cook in about five minutes.

2 tbsp extra virgin olive oil, plus extra for greasing
200g carrots, peeled and cut into thin sticks
2 large leeks (approx. 250g), trimmed and cut into thin strips
175g mangetout, trimmed and cut into thin strips
1 bunch of spring onions, cut into thin strips
4 eggs
4 tbsp fromage frais
salt and freshly ground black pepper

1. Preheat the oven to 200°C/Gas 6 and grease a shallow ovenproof dish.
2. Heat the oil in a large frying pan over a medium–high heat and stir-fry the carrots for 2–3 minutes. Add the rest of the vegetables and continue to stir-fry for another 2–3 minutes.
3. Spoon the vegetables into the prepared dish. Make four shallow hollows in the mixture. Break an egg into each hollow and top with a tablespoonful of fromage frais. Season the dish and bake for 10–15 minutes until the eggs are just set but the yolks are still runny. Serve hot.

VARIATIONS

Use carrots alone (you will need about 500g) and flavour with chopped fresh tarragon.

Use thinly sliced celery, green beans or spring greens instead of mangetout.

SOUFFLÉ MUSHROOMS

It is important to choose large open-cap mushrooms rather than flat field mushrooms, because the rim helps to stop the soufflé mixture from overflowing onto the baking sheet.

4 large open-cap mushrooms
extra virgin olive oil
75g grated cheese
25g fresh breadcrumbs
25g walnuts or pecan nuts, finely chopped
2 eggs, separated
1 tbsp thick soy sauce
1 tsp French mustard
salt and freshly ground black pepper

1. Preheat the oven to 200°C/Gas 6. Preheat the grill.
2. Cut the stalks out of the mushrooms. Brush the caps with olive oil and place under the grill, gill-side down. Cook for 5 minutes. Turn over and cook the other side for 5 minutes.
3. While the mushrooms are grilling, mix the cheese, breadcrumbs and nuts in a bowl. Mix in the egg yolks and all the remaining ingredients. This will make quite a stiff mixture.
4. Whisk the egg whites until they are very stiff. Mix 2 tablespoonfuls into the cheese mixture and then fold in the rest.
5. Place the grilled mushrooms in an ovenproof dish, gill-side up. Pile the cheese soufflé mixture on top. Place in the oven and bake for 10–15 minutes. Serve at once.

SPINACH BAKE WITH GOAT'S CHEESE

The idea for this recipe comes from Colombia. The yogurt, raisins and cinnamon give a sweet and spicy tang, which is typical of South American food.

450g frozen chopped spinach
50g raisins
200ml Greek-style yogurt
½ tsp ground cinnamon
salt and freshly ground black pepper
125g frozen (thawed) or canned sweetcorn
175g mature hard goat's cheese, grated
100g fresh breadcrumbs
knobs of butter

Garnish
chopped fresh chives

1. Preheat the oven to 220°C/Gas 7.
2. Put the spinach in a small saucepan with the raisins, yogurt, cinnamon, salt and pepper. Place over a medium heat and stir until the mixture comes to the boil. Cook for 4–5 minutes, stirring from time to time, until the liquid evaporates.
3. Spoon the mixture into an ovenproof dish and level the surface. Spread the sweetcorn over the top.
4. Mix the cheese and breadcrumbs and sprinkle over the corn. Dot with butter. Place in the oven and bake for 15 minutes until golden. Sprinkle with chopped chives and serve at once.

BAKED STUFFED TOMATOES
WITH CHICKPEAS (V)

Tomatoes cook relatively quickly, and in this dish the secret is to make sure that the filling is very hot before it goes into the tomatoes. Serve as a first course, or serve with other dishes, such as Egyptian-style rice (see page 218) and a green salad, to make a main meal.

You will need half a 400g can of chickpeas for this recipe. Use the leftover chickpeas in soup or toss with garlic, parsley and lemon juice and serve on a bed of rocket as a salad starter or lunch dish.

4 large ripe but firm tomatoes
2 tbsp extra virgin olive oil
1 onion, finely chopped
100g canned chickpeas, mashed or puréed in a food processor
3 tbsp chopped fresh coriander
salt and freshly ground black pepper

1. Preheat the oven to 200°C/Gas 6.
2. Slice the tops off the tomatoes and, using a knife or teaspoon, scoop out the seeds and soft flesh into a bowl. Keep the tops on one side. Discard any tough centres.
3. Heat the olive oil in a saucepan and fry the onion for 2–3 minutes until golden. Add the chickpeas, the tomato seed mixture, coriander, and salt and pepper to taste and heat through, stirring all the time.
4. Spoon this mixture into the prepared tomato shells and cover with the tops. Place on a baking sheet and bake for 15 minutes. Serve at once.

POLENTA PIE

This recipe comes from the Val d'Aosta in north-west Italy, where the local Fontina cheese would be used. It is a creamy semi-soft cheese which melts easily, but it is traditionally made with rennet. Philadelphia cream cheese is a good vegetarian substitute.

The secret of getting this recipe done quickly is to use ingredients that need little or no preparation before going into the pie. I have discovered a wonderful ready-made polenta that can be used straight from the pack. It comes in a thick sausage shape and you simply unpeel the wrapping and slice or mash with a fork depending upon the recipe. You can, of course, make your own polenta from scratch but you will need to buy the quick-cook variety, unless you have 45 minutes to stand and stir.

Cans of chopped tomatoes are ideal, too. Drain and keep the juices for use in soups and sauces.

extra virgin olive oil for greasing
400g can chopped tomatoes
salt and freshly ground black pepper
700g ready-made polenta, cut into 12 thick slices
200g Philadelphia cream cheese, cut into small pieces
freshly grated nutmeg
4 sprigs of basil, roughly chopped

1. Preheat the oven to 200°C/Gas 6 and brush a shallow ovenproof dish with oil.
2. Drain off the juices from the can of tomatoes and keep for another recipe. Put the tomatoes in a saucepan with the salt and pepper and bring to the boil.
3. Layer the slices of polenta in the dish with the tomatoes and cheese, seasoning and scatter with nutmeg and basil as you go. Finish with a layer of tomato.
4. Place in the oven and bake for 20 minutes until bubbling. Serve at once.

VARIATION

Top with a layer of grated Cheddar cheese.

BAKED STUFFED PEPPERS (V)

You can make these filled peppers as hot and spicy as you like, depending on your choice of curry powder or garam masala. Serve with Baked Stuffed Tomatoes with Chickpeas (see page 191) and noodles.

4 red or green peppers
4–5 tbsp vegetable stock

Stuffing
2 tbsp extra virgin olive oil
1 small onion, peeled and finely chopped
2 carrots, peeled and grated
200g canned red kidney beans, mashed or puréed in a food processor
1 cooking apple, cored and grated
1 tbsp mango chutney
1 tbsp curry powder or garam masala
salt and freshly ground black pepper

1. Preheat the oven to 200°C/Gas 6.
2. Slice the tops off the peppers and cut off the stalks; scrape all the seeds out of the centre of the peppers. Put the peppers into a large pan of boiling water and boil fast for about 7–8 minutes until just softened. Drain well on kitchen paper. Place in an ovenproof dish just large enough to hold the peppers upright.
3. Meanwhile, make the stuffing. Heat the olive oil in a saucepan and fry the onion until lightly browned. Add the carrots and cook for another 2–3 minutes.
4. Put the kidney beans in a bowl and add the onion, carrots and all the other stuffing ingredients. Season to taste, mix well and spoon into the prepared peppers.
5. Bring the stock to the boil and pour into the dish with the peppers. Place in the oven and bake for 15 minutes. Serve hot.

CHAPTER 11
PASTA AND NOODLE DISHES

Pasta and noodles are essential items for any store cupboard: they are quick to cook and extremely versatile, lending themselves to an almost infinite variety of sauces. They do not take up much space yet they expand to about three times their volume on cooking. Sauces can easily be made while the pasta is cooking.

Dried pasta cooks in about 5–10 minutes – partly depending on its shape – fresh pasta in 2–3 minutes. Some Chinese-style noodles are simply covered in boiling water and left to stand. Cook pasta in plenty of fast-boiling salted water. When cooked, the pasta should be 'al dente' or just firm to the bite. Follow the cooking time given on the pack, but you may want to test a piece just before that time, or you may need to cook for a minute longer.

Most of the recipes in this chapter specify the kind of pasta or noodles to use but there is no reason why you should not substitute other types. All recipes are for four people.

Grated Parmesan cheese is often added to pasta dishes, but Parmesan is made with animal rennet – and cheese cannot be labelled 'Parmesan' if it is not produced in the traditional region by the traditional method. Many producers now make Parmesan-style hard cheeses with vegetable rennet. Kosher Parmesan cheese comes into this category. Spenwood ewe's milk cheese is a Parmesan-type cheese; when mature it has a caramel flavour which is very good with pasta. Do not buy ready-grated cheese, it does not usually taste very good. Store cheese in a cool, dry place or, if your kitchen is quite warm, in the fridge.

SPAGHETTINI WITH PEAS AND HERBS

This is such a simple dish to make but it is truly delicious. It comes from the Veneto area of north-eastern Italy and I first tried it in a little restaurant just off the Grand Canal in Venice. It is essential to use butter, so don't be tempted to use margarine, or even a good olive oil. Spaghettini is simply thin spaghetti, so it is slightly quicker to cook.

450g fresh shelled peas, or frozen peas
75g butter, softened
4 tbsp chopped fresh parsley
4 tbsp chopped fresh basil
2 tbsp chopped fresh chives
1 garlic clove, peeled and crushed
350g spaghettini
salt and freshly ground black pepper
freshly grated Parmesan-style cheese

1. Steam the peas in a steamer or boil in a saucepan with very little water, for 5–8 minutes until just tender. If you are using frozen peas, cook as directed on the pack.
2. Put the butter in a bowl and mix in the herbs and garlic.
3. Cook the spaghettini in plenty of salted fast-boiling water until al dente.
4. Drain the pasta well and return to the hot pan. Add the peas and herb butter and toss well together. Serve at once with black pepper and grated cheese.

SPAGHETTI WITH ASPARAGUS

This is a delicately flavoured dish which is at its best in late spring when the English asparagus season is at its height. However, frozen asparagus can be quite good.

300g trimmed fresh or thawed frozen asparagus
150ml double cream
50ml well-flavoured vegetable stock
salt and freshly ground black pepper
350g spaghetti
1 tbsp extra virgin olive oil
4 tbsp freshly grated Parmesan-style cheese

1. Steam the asparagus for 5–6 minutes if using fresh asparagus, or about 3 minutes if using frozen, until just cooked through. Cut off the tips and keep on one side.
2. Purée the stalks in a blender or food processor with a little of the cream, or rub them through a sieve.
3. Put the purée in a saucepan, add the cream and stock and bring to the boil. Cook over a fairly high heat to reduce and thicken the sauce. Season to taste.
4. Meanwhile, cook the spaghetti in plenty of salted fast-boiling water until al dente. Drain and toss with the olive oil.
5. Pour the asparagus sauce over the pasta and toss well together. Garnish with the reserved asparagus tips and serve at once with the grated cheese and more black pepper.

SPAGHETTI WITH SUNFLOWER SEEDS AND SUN-DRIED TOMATOES

This sauce may seem a bit dry when you are making it, but it will be fine when mixed with the pasta, so avoid the temptation to add too much oil. Good herbs to use are sage, mint and thyme.

350g spaghetti
salt
50g sunflower seeds
40g sun-dried tomato paste
2 garlic cloves, crushed
freshly ground black pepper
a little extra virgin olive oil
a handful of fresh herbs, chopped or shredded
freshly grated Parmesan-style cheese

1. Cook the spaghetti in plenty of salted fast-boiling water until al dente.
2. While the pasta is cooking, toast the sunflower seeds in a non-stick frying pan until golden brown.
3. Leave the pan to cool slightly. Stir in the tomato paste, garlic, pepper and a little olive oil, depending on how much there is in the paste. Stir over a medium heat for about 1 minute.
4. When the pasta is cooked, drain it and tip it into a warmed serving bowl. Stir in the sauce and herbs. Serve at once with more olive oil and grated cheese.

SPAGHETTI WITH COURGETTES AND MINT

This recipe from Tuscany uses nepitella or wild mint. This is difficult to find in the UK and so I have used cultivated mint instead. However, our mint is much stronger in flavour and whereas the original recipe calls for a whole bunch of nepitella I use a few sprigs of English mint. The flavour is different, but it is still very good.

2 large garlic cloves
6 tbsp extra virgin olive oil
leaves from 4–5 sprigs of mint, coarsely shredded
4 small to medium courgettes, sliced
350g spaghetti
salt and freshly ground black pepper
freshly grated Parmesan-style cheese

1. Cut the garlic into quarters and place in a small bowl with 4 tablespoons of the oil. Add the mint and leave to stand until required.

2. Fry the courgettes in the remaining oil for about 8–10 minutes, stirring from time to time, until they are golden all over.

3. Meanwhile, cook the spaghetti in plenty of salted fast-boiling water until al dente. Drain well.

4. Remove the garlic from the oil and discard. Pour the oil and mint over the pasta and add the courgettes. Toss well and serve at once with black pepper and grated cheese.

TAGLIATELLE WITH TOASTED SEEDS AND PINE NUTS

This simple dish from the hills above Lake Garda in northern Italy has a wonderful flavour and an unusual texture. It can be made with cream or with a good extra virgin olive oil.

350g tagliatelle
salt
1 tsp extra virgin olive oil
2 tbsp pumpkin seeds
2 tbsp sunflower seeds
2 tbsp pine nuts
75ml double cream or extra virgin olive oil
freshly ground black pepper
freshly grated Parmesan-style cheese

1. Cook the pasta in plenty of fast-boiling salted water with 1 teaspoon of olive oil for 6–7 minutes or as directed on the pack, until al dente.
2. While the pasta is cooking, toast the seeds and pine nuts under a hot grill or in a hot dry frying pan until they are well browned but not burnt.
3. Drain the pasta well and toss with the toasted seeds and nuts and the cream or olive oil. Serve at once with plenty of black pepper and grated cheese.

FETTUCCINE WITH CARROT AND TARRAGON CARBONARA SAUCE

Carbonara should be a very creamy sauce, but if the eggs are overcooked it will be grainy. The eggs are added to the drained pasta and there should be enough heat in the pasta to cook them to the right consistency.

1 tbsp butter or extra virgin olive oil
2 carrots, peeled and very finely diced
1 tbsp very finely chopped shallots or onion
350g fettuccine
salt
3 large eggs, beaten
50g Parmesan-style cheese, grated, plus extra to serve
freshly ground black pepper
2 tbsp chopped fresh tarragon

1. Heat the butter or oil in a frying pan over a low–medium heat and gently fry the carrots and shallots or onion for about 6–7 minutes until tender.
2. Meanwhile, cook the fettuccine in plenty of salted fast-boiling water for about 7–8 minutes or as directed on the pack, until al dente.
3. Mix the eggs with the cheese, salt and pepper.
4. Drain the pasta and toss with the hot carrot mixture. Stir in the egg and cheese mixture, add the tarragon and toss well together. Serve at once with more black pepper and grated cheese.

PASTA WITH THREE-MUSHROOM CREAM SAUCE

A creamy and comforting pasta dish, served straight from the pan.

4 or 5 dried porcini mushrooms
25g pine nuts or flaked almonds
225g dried or fresh pasta, such as tagliatelle
salt
1 tsp extra virgin olive oil
50g butter
225g button mushrooms, sliced
100g oyster or chestnut mushrooms, sliced
150ml double cream
a pinch of freshly grated nutmeg
freshly ground black pepper

1. Put the dried mushrooms in a small bowl, pour in boiling water to just cover them and leave to stand for 10 minutes. Drain, cut off the stalks, discarding any tough parts, and slice the caps thinly.
2. Toast the pine nuts or almonds under a hot grill or in a hot dry frying pan.
3. Cook the pasta in plenty of salted fast-boiling water with 1 teaspoon of olive oil. Cook dried pasta for 8–10 minutes or fresh pasta for 2–3 minutes until al dente. Drain well and keep warm.
4. Melt the butter in a large frying pan and gently fry the three different kinds of mushroom together for about 3–4 minutes until they begin to soften.
5. Add the cream, nutmeg, salt and pepper and bring to the boil. Add the pasta and toss well together. Sprinkle with the toasted nuts and serve at once.

PASTA WITH LEEK AND GARLIC SAUCE

You can use any kind of garlic-flavoured soft cheese for this quickie; Boursin or garlic roulade work well. Serve with chunky pasta shapes such as penne, rigatoni or fusilli.

350g pasta
salt
3–4 leeks, trimmed and thickly sliced
150g Boursin cheese
3 tbsp double cream
2 tbsp chopped fresh parsley
freshly ground black pepper

1. Cook the pasta in plenty of salted fast-boiling water until al dente.
2. While the pasta is cooking, steam the leeks for 5–8 minutes until softened but still with a bite.
3. Heat the cheese with the cream in a small saucepan, stirring until all the cheese has melted. Bring to the boil and remove from the heat.
4. Stir in the leeks, parsley and pepper. Drain the pasta, pour the sauce over and serve at once.

TAGLIOLINI WITH BROCCOLI PESTO

You can make this lovely pasta dish with cauliflower instead of broccoli but the latter is more colourful. Save the stalks and use in any of the mixed vegetable casseroles or curries in Chapter 7.

225g dried tagliolini or long thin flat pasta
salt

Broccoli pesto
350g broccoli
4 large sprigs of basil
1 large garlic clove, peeled and chopped
75g pine nuts
150ml extra virgin olive oil
75g Parmesan-style cheese, grated
salt and freshly ground black pepper

1. To make the broccoli pesto, cut the florets from the stalks of broccoli and place in a blender or food processor with the basil, garlic and pine nuts. Process until smooth. Stir in the olive oil and the cheese and season to taste.
2. Cook the pasta in plenty of salted fast-boiling water until al dente. Drain well, return to the pan and toss with the broccoli pesto. Serve at once.

RAVIOLI WITH SAGE AND COURGETTES

This simple Roman recipe makes an excellent supper dish served with a rocket salad. In Rome this would be made with spinach and ricotta-filled ravioli but you can choose any vegetarian ravioli. Any well-flavoured hard cheese can be used to sprinkle over the pasta.

25g butter
450g courgettes, thinly sliced
450g fresh ravioli
salt
75ml single cream
leaves from 4 small sprigs of sage
freshly ground black pepper
125g well-flavoured hard cheese, grated

1. Heat the butter in a frying pan and gently fry the courgettes for 5–6 minutes until softened but not browned.
2. Cook the ravioli in plenty of salted boiling water for 3–5 minutes or as directed on the pack.
3. Pour the cream over the courgettes and add the sage leaves, salt and pepper. Bring to the boil and simmer gently for 2–3 minutes. Take care not to boil off too much of the cream.
4. Drain the ravioli and layer on serving dishes with the courgette and cream mixture. Serve at once with the cheese sprinkled over the top.

PASTA SHELLS WITH FRESH BEANS AND TOMATO SAUCE (V)

Many pasta dishes need a little cheese to complement their flavour, but this one is very good on its own.

225g dried pasta shells
salt
175g frozen broad beans
175g green beans, topped and tailed and cut into 4cm lengths
2 tbsp extra virgin olive oil
400g can chopped tomatoes
1 tsp dried oregano
freshly ground black pepper

1. Cook the pasta shells in plenty of salted fast-boiling water until al dente.
2. Meanwhile, cook the frozen beans in lightly salted boiling water as directed on the pack. Add the green beans about 4 minutes before the end of the cooking time. Drain well.
3. Heat the olive oil in a deep saucepan and add the tomatoes, oregano, salt and pepper and bring to the boil. Cook over a high heat for 4–5 minutes, stirring from time to time. Stir in the beans.
4. Drain the pasta shells well and turn into a deep bowl. Pour the bean and tomato mixture over the top. Toss and serve at once.

PASTA BOWS WITH GOAT'S CHEESE SAUCE

As well as providing extra flavour, the seeds add an unusual crunchy texture to this sauce. Poppy seeds are a popular flavouring for both sweet and savoury dishes in Hungary, as are sesame seeds in the Middle East.

1 tbsp poppy seeds or sesame seeds
350g pasta bows
salt
2 tbsp extra virgin olive oil
1 onion, peeled and finely chopped
4 tbsp dry white wine
2 tbsp vegetable stock
175g fresh goat's cheese, cut into small chunks
freshly ground black pepper
freshly grated hard goat's cheese

1. Toast the poppy seeds or sesame seeds in a dry frying pan over a medium heat for about 1 minute. Keep on one side.
2. Cook the pasta in plenty of salted fast-boiling water for 7–8 minutes or until al dente.
3. Meanwhile, heat the olive oil in a saucepan and gently fry the onion for 2–3 minutes until softened but not browned.
4. Add the wine and stock and bring to the boil, then reduce the heat and stir in the soft cheese. When the cheese has melted, stir in the seeds and pepper and heat through.
5. Drain the pasta and toss together with the sauce. Serve at once with more pepper and the grated hard cheese.

FUSILLI WITH WILD MUSHROOMS AND CANNELLINI BEANS (V)

This pasta dish comes from Verona in northern Italy. It is usually served in the autumn, when fresh porcini mushrooms (ceps) are in season, but I make it all the year round, using dried mushrooms.

15g dried porcini mushrooms
4 tbsp extra virgin olive oil
1 small onion, peeled and coarsely chopped
2 garlic cloves, crushed
1 small carrot, peeled and diced
2 sticks of celery, trimmed and diced
225g canned or cooked cannellini beans
2 tbsp dry white wine
1 tsp tomato purée
salt and freshly ground black pepper
350g fusilli
leaves from 1 sprig of sage, chopped

1. Put the mushrooms in a small bowl and add just enough boiling water to cover them. Leave to soak for about 15 minutes while you prepare the vegetables.
2. Heat half the olive oil in a saucepan and fry the onion and garlic for 3–4 minutes until lightly browned. Add the carrots and celery and cook for 3–4 minutes.
3. Add the cannellini beans to the pan, together with the mushrooms and their soaking water, the wine, tomato purée, salt and pepper. Bring to the boil and simmer for 10 minutes until the vegetables are just cooked.
4. Meanwhile, cook the pasta in plenty of salted fast-boiling water until al dente.
5. Drain the pasta and toss with the remaining olive oil and the sage. Add the cooked vegetables, toss together and serve at once.

FRIED EGG NOODLES

This is my simplified version of an Indonesian noodle dish. It can be served with almost any of the recipes in the Stir-fries and Wok Cookery chapter (see pages 161–76).

2 tbsp extra virgin olive oil
2 eggs, beaten
225g Chinese egg noodles
salt
1 garlic clove, crushed
2 lumps of stem ginger or 3 cm fresh root ginger, finely chopped
1 onion, finely chopped
2 sticks of celery, finely sliced
1 tbsp soy sauce
2 tbsp dry sherry
1 bunch of spring onions, sliced lengthways

1. Heat 1 tablespoon of the oil in a large frying pan over a medium–high heat and pour in the beaten eggs. Allow the eggs to spread out to make a large flat omelette. When cooked through, remove from the pan and cut into strips. Keep warm.
2. Cook the noodles in plenty of salted boiling water for 5 minutes or as directed on the pack. Drain and keep on one side.
3. Meanwhile, heat the remaining oil in the frying pan and stir-fry the garlic, ginger, onion and celery for about 5–8 minutes until tender.
4. Add the soy sauce, sherry and the noodles. Heat through, stirring well. Serve at once, garnished with sliced spring onions and the omelette strips.

SINGAPORE NOODLES (V)

Every Chinese restaurant I have ever been to seems to have its own recipe for Singapore Noodles. They often include non-vegetarian ingredients, but the one thing they all have in common is red chillies. The basic recipe makes an excellent accompaniment to stir-fries and dishes such as Chickpeas with Spinach (see page 122) or Tagine of Okra and Tomatoes (see page 124). Alternatively, add any or all of the optional extras to make a more interesting noodle dish.

225g Chinese egg noodles
1 tbsp groundnut oil
225g bean sprouts
1 tsp soy sauce
½ tsp curry powder
2–3 fresh red chillies, seeded and very finely sliced

Optional extras
1 tsp roasted sesame oil
2 tbsp cooked peas
2 tbsp cooked sweetcorn
2 tbsp diced bamboo shoots
50g mangetout, blanched in boiling water for 1 minute, then drained
1 bunch of spring onions, sliced in half lengthways

1. Cook the noodles in plenty of salted boiling water for 5 minutes or as directed on the pack. Drain well.
2. Heat the oil in a wok or large frying pan over a high heat and toss the bean sprouts in the oil. Add the noodles, the soy sauce and curry powder, along with any optional extras, and toss well together until heated through. Add the chillies and serve at once.

JAPANESE BUCKWHEAT NOODLES WITH TAMARI, GINGER AND SPRING ONIONS (V)

Japanese buckwheat (soba) noodles can be used in much the same way as Chinese egg noodles. They have quite a strong taste of their own and need punchy flavours to go with them.

300g Japanese buckwheat noodles
2 tbsp groundnut oil
2 tbsp grated fresh root ginger
2 garlic cloves, peeled and crushed
2–3 spring onions, finely chopped
3 tbsp tamari sauce
freshly ground black pepper

1. Prepare the noodles as directed on the pack.
2. Meanwhile, heat the oil in a wok or deep frying pan and add the ginger, garlic and spring onions. Stir-fry for 2 minutes.
3. Add the drained noodles and stir-fry for another minute or so. Add the tamari sauce and pepper and bring to the boil. Serve at once.

VEGETABLE NOODLES
WITH NUT SAUCE (V)

Peanut butter is the obvious choice for this recipe but other nut butters are available in health food shops and delicatessens. Look out for cashew, walnut or almond butter. You can also use tahini (sesame seed paste). The recipe works well with any kind of noodles: Chinese egg or rice noodles, Japanese buckwheat (soba) noodles, Italian pasta.

250g noodles
salt
4 tbsp groundnut oil
1 onion, peeled and finely chopped
2 tbsp nut butter
3 tbsp orange juice
100ml vegetable stock
salt and freshly ground black pepper
½ tsp coriander seeds
225g carrots, peeled and coarsely grated
175g celeriac, kohlrabi or parsnips, coarsely grated
1 tsp grated orange zest
1–2 tbsp soy sauce

1. Cook the noodles in salted boiling water as directed on the pack.

2. Meanwhile, heat half the oil in a saucepan and fry the onion for a couple of minutes until softened. Stir in the nut butter, orange juice and stock, adding the stock gradually to make a smooth paste. Heat the mixture through, but take care not to overcook or it will thicken. However, if this does happen simply add more stock. Season.

3. Heat the remaining oil in a wok or deep frying pan and fry the coriander seeds for a minute until they start to pop. Add the grated vegetables and stir-fry for 1–2 minutes.

4. Drain the noodles and add to the pan with the vegetables. Toss well together over a high heat. Add the orange zest and soy sauce and spoon onto serving plates. Top with the nut sauce and serve at once.

WARM SPICY NOODLE SALAD
WITH WATER CHESTNUTS (V)

Chinese thread egg noodles are very thin and are the best choice
for this dish but you can use any kind of quick-cook egg noodles.

280g dried Chinese thread egg noodles
1 large green pepper, seeded and thinly shredded
1 large bunch of spring onions, sliced thinly on the slant
225g can water chestnuts, drained and sliced
2–3 tbsp light soy sauce
2 tsp roasted sesame oil
juice of ½ lemon
1 tbsp sake or dry sherry (optional)
1 tsp grated fresh root ginger
freshly ground black pepper

1. Put the noodles in a bowl and cover with boiling water.
   Leave to stand for 5–8 minutes or as directed on the pack.
2. Prepare all the vegetables and keep on one side.
3. Beat 2 tablespoons of the soy sauce with the sesame oil,
   lemon juice, sake or sherry if using, grated ginger and
   pepper.
4. Drain the noodles well and toss with the prepared vegetables and
   then with the soy sauce mixture. Leave to stand for 5 minutes.
5. Taste the noodles to see if they need any more seasoning.
   You may need to add a little more soy sauce. Serve at once.

CHAPTER 12
RICE AND GRAIN DISHES

Rice and cereals such as quinoa, bulgur wheat and polenta are excellent convenience foods. They are all very easy to cook in about double their volume of boiling liquid; by the time they have absorbed the liquid they should be ready to serve.

Cooking times for the rice dishes are based on long-grain white rice. If you prefer to use brown rice you will need to add a little more cooking liquid and to increase the cooking time by about 5–10 minutes. The bulgur recipes all use quick-cook bulgur rather than cracked wheat, which can take longer to cook. Always check the instructions on the pack.

Some of the recipes in this chapter are main courses in their own right, perhaps served with a salad or a simple vegetable dish. Others are designed as an accompaniment to other main-course dishes. All recipes are for four people.

TURKISH-STYLE RICE (V)

This wonderfully aromatic dish is good enough to eat on its own or you can serve it with many of the other dishes in this book.

2½ tbsp extra virgin olive oil, plus 1 tsp to serve
1 small onion, very finely chopped
225g long-grain rice
1 tsp salt
a good grinding of black pepper
2 tbsp pistachio nuts, chopped
1 tbsp cashew nuts (optional), roughly chopped
25g raisins
1 tbsp chopped fresh parsley
½ tbsp chopped fresh sage
½ tbsp chopped fresh mint
¼ tsp mixed spice
450ml vegetable stock

1. Heat the oil in a large saucepan. Add the onion and rice and fry gently for 2 minutes, stirring all the time. Add all the remaining ingredients except the stock and continue frying and stirring for another 3 minutes.
2. Pour in the stock and bring to the boil. Cover with a lid and cook over the lowest possible heat for 15 minutes or until the rice is tender and all the liquid has been absorbed.
3. Remove the pan from the heat and leave to stand for 5 minutes. Add a teaspoon of olive oil and serve.

MEXICAN-STYLE RICE (V)

This spicy rice dish is so good I often eat it on its own with a green salad, but it is also very good with grilled burgers or kebabs.

2 tbsp extra virgin olive oil
225g long-grain rice
400g can chopped tomatoes
300ml vegetable stock
1 tsp chilli powder (or to taste)
salt and freshly ground black pepper
1 red and 1 green pepper, sliced in rings, seeded
1 onion, peeled and thinly sliced

1. Heat the oil in a large saucepan and fry the rice for 2 minutes, stirring all the time. Pour in the tomatoes, stock, chilli powder and salt and pepper. Bring to the boil and stir.
2. Lay the peppers and onion on top of the rice. Cover with a lid and leave to cook over the lowest possible heat for 15 minutes or until the rice is tender and all the liquid has been absorbed. Serve at once.

EGYPTIAN-STYLE RICE (V)

Rice is popular in Egypt but the spicing is quite different to that used in other parts of the Eastern Mediterranean. I happily eat this on its own with a simple green salad, but you can also serve it with falafel and a tomato salad, or one of the simpler stir-fries in Chapter 9.

3 tbsp extra virgin olive oil
1 onion, peeled and finely chopped
1 garlic clove, peeled and chopped
1 tbsp chopped fresh coriander
1 tbsp chopped fresh basil (optional)
1 tsp turmeric
1 tsp dried thyme
½ tsp cayenne pepper
50g raisins, chopped
50g almonds, chopped
225g long-grain rice
450ml water
salt and freshly ground black pepper
50g vermicelli or spaghetti

1. Heat half the oil in a heavy-based saucepan and fry the onion until golden brown.
2. Add all the remaining ingredients except the vermicelli and the rest of the oil. Bring to the boil, stir and cover with a lid.
3. Reduce the heat and simmer for 15 minutes until the rice is tender and all the liquid has been absorbed.
4. Meanwhile, break the vermicelli into short lengths and cook in plenty of salted boiling water for about 6–8 minutes until tender. Drain very well and dry thoroughly. Heat the remaining oil in a small pan and fry the cooked vermicelli until golden.
5. Fluff up the cooked rice with a fork and stir in the fried vermicelli. Serve at once.

EGG AND CARDAMOM PILAF
WITH CARROTS

This pilaf can be served as a main course, with a simple green salad on the side.

4 onions, peeled
4 tbsp extra virgin olive oil
225g long-grain rice
2 carrots, peeled and coarsely grated
2 tbsp raisins
450ml vegetable stock
1 tbsp finely chopped parsley
1 tbsp finely chopped mint
salt and freshly ground black pepper
6 eggs
seeds from 3–4 cardamom pods

1. Very finely chop two of the onions and keep the rest on one side.
2. Heat half the olive oil in a saucepan and fry the chopped onions until softened but not browned. Add the rice and fry for 1–2 minutes, stirring all the time.
3. Add the carrots, raisins, stock, herbs, salt and pepper. Bring to the boil, cover with a lid and simmer until all the liquid has been absorbed. Remove from the heat and stir. Replace the lid and leave to stand in a warm place for 10 minutes.
4. Hard-boil the eggs, peel and slice. Slice the remaining onions into rings.
5. Heat the remaining oil in a frying pan over a high heat and fry the cardamom seeds for 30 seconds. Add the onion rings and fry until they are brown but still crisp.
6. Fluff up the cooked rice with a fork and pile onto warmed plates. Top with the sliced hard-boiled eggs and onion rings and serve at once.

RICE WITH PEPPERS (V)

This simple rice dish from the Extremadura region is typical of the resourcefulness of regional cooking in the poorer areas of Spain. It is traditionally prepared in large quantities with whole peppers, but the peppers can also be cut into quarters as I have suggested here.

3 tbsp extra virgin olive oil
½ small onion, peeled and chopped
225g long-grain rice
2 small green peppers, seeded and cut into quarters
1 red pepper, seeded and cut into quarters
a few strands of saffron
salt and ground white pepper
475ml water

1. Heat the olive oil in a saucepan and fry the onion until golden. Add the rice and fry for 1–2 minutes, stirring all the time with a wooden spoon.
2. Add the green and red peppers, saffron, salt and pepper.
3. Pour in the water and bring to the boil. Reduce the heat, cover with a lid and simmer for 15 minutes until the rice is tender and all the liquid has been absorbed. Serve at once.

EMPEDRADO MADRILENO (V)

This dish gets its name from the old method of dry-stone building of houses in Spain. Small pebbles or gravel were pushed into the cracks between the stones. It is said that the red beans resemble the stones and the rice is like the gravel inserts.

400g can borlotti or red kidney beans, drained
75g long-grain rice
2 onions, peeled and chopped
1 garlic clove, peeled and chopped
1 bay leaf
a pinch of salt
175ml water
2 tbsp extra virgin olive oil
1 tbsp paprika

1. Put the beans and rice in a saucepan and stir in half the onion, the garlic, bay leaf and salt.
2. Pour in the water and bring to the boil. Stir once and cover with a lid. Reduce the heat and simmer for 12 minutes until the rice is tender and all the liquid has been absorbed.
3. Meanwhile, heat the oil in a frying pan and fry the remaining onion with the paprika for 4 minutes until lightly browned.
4. Stir the fried onion into the beans and rice and cook for another 5 minutes. Serve at once.

SPICY CORN PILAF (V)

A friend of mine is addicted to Tabasco sauce and sweetcorn and this is one of her creations. It's a piquant rice dish which goes well with the Banana Kebabs (see page 154).

2 tbsp extra virgin olive oil
1 onion, peeled and chopped
225g long-grain rice
75g fresh or frozen sweetcorn kernels
½ small red pepper, seeded and finely chopped
1 tsp ground cinnamon
1 tbsp chopped fresh mixed herbs
5–6 drops of Tabasco sauce
salt and freshly ground black pepper
350ml vegetable stock or water

1. Heat the oil in a saucepan and fry the onion until lightly browned. Add the rice and stir well.
2. Add all the other ingredients and bring the mixture to the boil. Stir once and reduce the heat. Cover with a lid and simmer for 15 minutes until the rice is tender and all the liquid has been absorbed. Serve at once.

CARIBBEAN BANANA RICE (V)

This is very good served sprinkled with toasted pine nuts.

2 tbsp extra virgin olive oil
a few drops of roasted sesame oil
1 bunch of spring onions, chopped
2.5cm piece of fresh root ginger, peeled and grated
½ tsp ground allspice
1 fresh green chilli, seeded and finely sliced
225g risotto rice
550ml vegetable stock
salt and freshly ground black pepper
1 large banana, peeled and diced

1. Heat the olive oil with the sesame oil in a saucepan and gently fry the spring onions and ginger for 2–3 minutes.
2. Add the allspice, chilli and rice. Stir well and add half the stock. Bring to the boil and cook for about 10 minutes, uncovered, stirring from time to time. Add a little more stock if the mixture becomes very dry.
3. Add the rest of the stock and the seasoning and bring back to the boil. Continue to cook for about 10 minutes, then stir in the banana and cook for a further 5 minutes until all the liquid has been absorbed and the rice is quite creamy. Serve at once.

BULGUR AND NUT PILAF (V)

Make sure that you buy quick-cook bulgur. Some types – sometimes labelled cracked wheat – can be slow to cook. Quinoa is also very good cooked in this way. Serve with a tossed salad.

2 tbsp extra virgin olive oil
1 small onion, peeled and chopped
1 small green pepper, seeded and chopped
125g canned or cooked red kidney beans
50g cashew nuts, toasted under the grill
175g bulgur wheat
100ml vegetable stock
salt and freshly ground black pepper

1. Heat the oil in a saucepan and fry the onion for 2–3 minutes. Add the green pepper and cook for a further 1–2 minutes.
2. Add all the remaining ingredients and bring to the boil, stir and cover with a lid.
3. Reduce the heat and simmer for 11–15 minutes until the bulgur is cooked and all the liquid has been absorbed. Fluff up with a fork and serve.

BULGUR WITH FRESH HERBS (V)

This is like a hot version of tabbouleh salad, though the ratio of bulgur to parsley is higher. It is delicious on its own or served with kebabs.

2 tbsp extra virgin olive oil
½ bunch of spring onions, chopped
1 tomato, skinned, seeded and chopped
6 tbsp chopped fresh parsley
1 tbsp chopped fresh mint
225g bulgur wheat
salt and freshly ground black pepper
150ml vegetable stock

1. Heat the oil in a saucepan and gently fry the spring onions for 2–3 minutes.
2. Stir in the chopped tomato and herbs and then add the bulgur, seasoning and stock. Bring to the boil, stir and cover with a lid.
3. Reduce the heat and simmer for 11–15 minutes until the bulgur is cooked and all the liquid has been absorbed. Fluff up with a fork and serve.

SIX JEWEL RICE (V)

The six jewels are the vegetables which give the colour to this attractive rice dish. If you do not have exactly these vegetables use whatever you have to hand or simply make five or even four jewel rice!

500ml vegetable stock
1 red pepper, seeded and diced
1 small carrot, peeled and very finely diced
2 small courgettes, diced
50g frozen sweetcorn
50g frozen peas
100g mushrooms, diced
225g long-grain rice
½ tsp dried mixed herbs
salt and freshly ground black pepper

1. Bring the stock to the boil. Prepare all the vegetables and mix with the rice, herbs and seasoning. Place in a large saucepan and cover with the boiling vegetable stock. Stir once and bring back to the boil.

2. Cover with a lid, reduce the heat and simmer for 15 minutes. Check to see if all the liquid has been absorbed. If not, cook for a further 5 minutes.

3. Leave to stand for a minute or two, then fluff up with a fork and serve.

VARIATIONS

Top with crumbled smoked tofu and freshly chopped herbs to make a nutritious main course.

Non-vegans may like to add scrambled eggs and spring onion flowers. Spring onion flowers are a classic Chinese garnish: to make them, slice a spring onion lengthways several times, without slicing all the way through the end of the bulb. Place in a bowl of cold water; the spring onion will curl open to make a flower-like shape.

EASTERN FRIED RICE WITH CELERIAC (V)

You can use any root vegetable in this unusual rice dish; it was inspired by an old recipe I came across in my mother's scrapbook many years ago. I have tried it with parsnips, carrots and mooli (daikon) and they all work very well.

200g long-grain rice
1 small onion, peeled and finely chopped
1 stick of celery, finely chopped
2 tbsp flaked almonds, toasted
salt and freshly ground black pepper
400ml boiling water
2 tbsp extra virgin olive oil
225g celeriac, peeled and cut into thin sticks
2 garlic cloves, peeled and crushed
3 tbsp chopped fresh coriander
grated zest of 1 lemon
½ tsp minced chilli in oil or a few drops of Tabasco sauce

1. Mix the rice, onion, celery, almonds, salt and pepper in a saucepan and add the boiling water. Bring to the boil, stir and cover with a lid. Reduce the heat and simmer for 12–15 minutes until the rice is tender and all the liquid has been absorbed.
2. Meanwhile, heat the olive oil in a wok or deep frying pan and add the celeriac. Stir-fry over a medium heat for 2–3 minutes.
3. Mix the garlic, coriander, lemon zest and chilli or Tabasco together in a cup. Keep on one side.
4. Add the cooked rice to the celeriac and stir-fry for about a minute. Add the garlic mixture and stir-fry for another 2–3 minutes. Serve at once.

RICE WITH PUMPKIN AND PEAS (V)

This Mexican-inspired dish makes a good main course served with a salad. It can also be served with any kind of casserole or with stuffed or grilled vegetables. You can vary the amount of chilli you use to suit your own palate or to go with your chosen accompaniment.

1 tbsp extra virgin olive oil
1 small onion, peeled and finely chopped
2 garlic cloves, peeled and crushed
225g long-grain rice
1 green pepper, seeded and chopped
2 green chillies, seeded and finely chopped
175g peeled and seeded pumpkin, finely diced
75g fresh or frozen peas
500ml vegetable stock
salt and freshly ground black pepper

1. Heat the oil in a saucepan over a medium heat and fry the onion and garlic for about 3–4 minutes until lightly browned. Add the rice and stir well.
2. Add all the remaining ingredients and bring to the boil. Stir and cover with a lid. Reduce the heat and cook for 15 minutes until the rice is tender and all the liquid has been absorbed. Fluff up with a fork and serve at once.

VARIATIONS

Stir in four or five finely chopped spring onions just before serving.
Add some toasted nuts to add extra protein.

BULGUR WHEAT WITH OKRA (V)

This filling Middle Eastern dish is delicious with a simple side salad. It also goes well with most of the casseroles and curries in Chapter 7. You can use fresh or frozen okra; either way, choose very small or baby okra.

200g bulgur wheat
250g fresh or frozen very small or baby okra
3 tbsp extra virgin olive oil
1 large onion, peeled and finely chopped
1 large red pepper, seeded and finely chopped
2 tomatoes, skinned and chopped
4 tbsp dry white wine or vegetable stock
salt and freshly ground black pepper
6–8 sprigs of coriander

1. Put the bulgur in a bowl and add boiling water to cover by about 2cm. Leave to stand for at least 10 minutes. It should swell and absorb most of the water.

2. Put the okra in a saucepan and cover with boiling water. Bring back to the boil and simmer for about 3–4 minutes until softened.

3. Heat the olive oil in a frying pan and fry the onion and pepper for 2–3 minutes. Add the tomatoes and wine or stock and cook for a further 3–4 minutes, stirring from time to time.

4. Drain the okra and the bulgur wheat and dry them both on kitchen paper. Add to the pan with the onion and tomato mixture. Season well and cook over a high heat for about 5–6 minutes, turning the mixture when it begins to brown on the base. Serve garnished with sprigs of coriander.

POLENTA RUSTICA

Look for quick-cooking cornmeal or polenta: it is ready in minutes and there is no need to stand over it stirring. In the Val d'Aosta in north-west Italy polenta is a staple food and it is often flavoured with the local Fontina cheese. Serve with rocket or a mixed green salad for a rich and filling supper.

225g fast-cooking polenta or cornmeal
600–750ml water
salt
50g soft blue cheese, diced
75g Brie-style cheese with rind removed, diced
50g butter
freshly ground black pepper

1. Prepare the polenta as directed on the pack, with about 600ml of salted water. Add more water if the mixture gets very thick.
2. After about 4–5 minutes, add the cheeses. As soon as the cheese has melted and blended with the polenta, stir in the butter. Season to taste and serve hot.

CHAPTER 13
VEGETABLE ACCOMPANIMENTS

This chapter offers some unusual alternative side dishes. All are designed to preserve the maximum amount of nutrients from the vegetables in the finished dish.

The best way to cook plain vegetable accompaniments is to steam them or to poach them in olive oil. The recipe for Peppers Poached in Olive Oil would also work well with cauliflower florets, chunks of courgette, diced pumpkin or butternut squash. I rarely boil vegetables in water; all the water-soluble vitamins leach out and are lost in the cooking liquor. If you do decide that boiling is the speediest cooking method, keep the cooking liquor to use in soups and sauces. This also applies to steaming water.

The recipes in this section are designed to be served as side dishes; all are for four people.

CHILLI-BRAISED CABBAGE (V)

Cabbage can form the basis of a wide range of interesting dishes. This one comes from Hungary, where hot paprika pepper is used. It is quite difficult to find outside Hungary so I have used fresh green chilli for heat and a mild paprika for the flavour.

2 tbsp extra virgin olive oil
1 large onion, peeled and sliced
1 green chilli, seeded and chopped
½ head of white cabbage, shredded
4 large tomatoes, skinned and chopped
2 tsp paprika
juice of 1 lime
75ml vegetable stock
salt and freshly ground black pepper

1. Heat the oil in a large saucepan and fry the onion and chilli for 4–5 minutes until lightly browned. Add the remaining ingredients and bring to the boil.
2. Cook over a medium heat, stirring from time to time, for about 8–10 minutes until just tender. Serve hot.

PEPPERS POACHED IN OLIVE OIL (V)

This is a wonderful combination of ingredients: research has shown that the nutrients from the peppers together with those from the olive oil give more health benefits than cooking the two ingredients separately.

1 red pepper
1 green pepper
1 orange or yellow pepper
100ml extra virgin olive oil

1. Cut the peppers into quarters and remove all the membranes and seeds. Cut each quarter into two pieces.
2. Pour the olive oil into a large frying pan with a lid and arrange the peppers in the pan so that they do not overlap. Put the pan over a low–medium heat and watch until the oil just starts to sizzle. Turn the heat down as low as it will go and cover the pan with a lid.
3. Cook very slowly for about 25 minutes until the peppers are tender. Check from time to time to ensure that the peppers continue to cook gently but do not sizzle. Serve hot or cold, with the cooking juices.

OKRA WITH COCONUT (V)

This is quite a dry dish from southern India. Choose the smallest and youngest okra pods you can find as they will be much more tender and less stringy and gelatinous than older ones. From time to time my local Middle Eastern greengrocer has tiny okra that are about 1–2cm long and they are delicious cooked this way.

2 tbsp extra virgin olive oil
seeds from 3 cardamom pods
¼ tsp yellow mustard seeds (optional)
1 small onion, peeled and very finely chopped
½ tsp turmeric
225g baby okra, sliced across the pods
15g desiccated coconut
4 tbsp chopped fresh coriander to garnish

1. Heat the oil in a large saucepan and fry the seeds until they pop. Add the onion and fry for 1–2 minutes.
2. Add all the remaining ingredients except the coriander and fry for about 6–8 minutes, stirring all the time, until the okra is tender but still retains its shape. Serve hot, garnished with fresh coriander.

GRATED POTATO CAKES

Serve this variation on Jewish latkes with a casserole (see Chapter 7) or another of the vegetable dishes from this chapter, or enjoy as a tasty snack with apple sauce.

½ small onion, peeled
600g potatoes, peeled
2 large eggs
3 tbsp plain flour
4 tbsp chopped fresh dill
salt and freshly ground black pepper
4 tbsp extra virgin olive oil

1. Grate the onion into a large bowl and then grate in the potato. Mix with the eggs as quickly as possible to stop the potatoes discolouring. Stir in the flour, dill, salt and pepper.
2. Heat the oil in a large frying pan. Drop 8 tablespoonfuls of the mixture into the hot fat and spread out so that they are fairly thin (thicker cakes will take longer to cook).
3. Cook over a medium heat for about 8–10 minutes on each side. They should be well browned on the outside and soft in the middle. Serve hot.

VARIATION
Use 2 tablespoons mustard and 1 tablespoon creamed horseradish in place of the dill.

SHAKEN PEAS

The name of this dish is said to come from the eighteenth-century pan which was used to cook it – a shaking pan. I think it must have been the equivalent of our frying pan and that is what I use to cook the dish. The sauce is quite thin, so if you prefer a thicker sauce, mix ½ teaspoon of cornflour with 2 teaspoons of cold water and mix into the soured cream, and add a little more seasoning.

2 tbsp extra virgin olive oil
1 onion, peeled and thinly sliced
1 garlic clove, peeled and crushed
350g frozen peas
½ Cos lettuce, shredded
4 tbsp soured cream
2 tbsp dry white wine or vegetable stock
leaves from 4 large sprigs of mint, chopped
salt and ground white pepper

1. Heat the oil in a small deep-sided frying pan. Add the onion and garlic and cook over a low heat until softened but not browned.
2. Add the peas and shake or stir the pan until the peas thaw. Continue to cook over a low heat for about 2–3 minutes, stirring occasionally.
3. Add all the remaining ingredients and bring to the boil. Simmer for another minute or so and then serve at once.

VARIATION
Use freshly chopped chervil or parsley in place of mint.

BEETROOT WITH APPLES (V)

In this dish from central Russia, the sweetness of the beetroot balances the sourness of the cooking apple and the two are complemented by the ginger.

450g raw beetroot, peeled and grated
200ml vegetable stock
1 large cooking apple, cored and grated
1 tsp grated fresh root ginger
salt and freshly ground black pepper
1 tbsp cider vinegar

1. Put the grated beetroot in a saucepan with the stock and bring to the boil. Cover with a lid and cook over a low heat for about 15 minutes.
2. Add the apple, ginger, salt and pepper and cook for another 5 minutes.
3. Add the vinegar and turn up the heat to boil off the excess liquid, stirring frequently to avoid burning. Serve hot.

VARIATIONS

This dish is often cooked with 3–4 tablespoons soured cream stirred in at the end and gently heated. The result is much richer and is delicious served with plainly grilled vegetables.

Alternatively, cook the beetroot with the juice of 1 orange, a little grated orange zest and a knob of butter instead of the stock. Omit the cider vinegar.

BRUSSELS SPROUTS
WITH NUTMEG BREADCRUMBS

These crunchy-coated sprouts are inspired by dishes I have eaten in Holland and Hungary. Steamed sprouts sprinkled with nutmeg are popular in Holland and I enjoyed Brussels sprouts with a breadcrumb dressing at a restaurant in central Hungary. The flavour is very much better if made with butter, but a good extra virgin olive oil can be used if you need to avoid dairy products.

450g Brussels sprouts
75g butter or 5 tbsp extra virgin olive oil
125g fresh breadcrumbs
½ tsp freshly grated nutmeg
salt

1. Cook the sprouts in a steamer for about 20 minutes until just tender, then drain.
2. Meanwhile, melt the butter or heat the oil in a frying pan and add the breadcrumbs. Fry over a medium heat until well browned. Mix in the nutmeg and a little salt.
3. Add the drained sprouts to the pan and turn them around until they are well coated with crispy breadcrumbs. Serve at once.

VARIATION

Fry some finely chopped nuts with the breadcrumbs. Try pecan nuts, walnuts or peanuts.

GINGERED NEEPS

In Scotland 'neeps' usually refers to large yellow/pink swedes rather than to small white turnips, and swede is the best vegetable to use in this unusual recipe. Don't stint on the butter, it really is essential for the very best results.

450g swede, peeled and diced
25g butter
2 cloves
½ bunch of spring onions, finely chopped
1 tbsp grated fresh root ginger
salt and ground white pepper

1. Cook the swede in a steamer for 15–20 minutes until just tender.
2. Melt the butter in a saucepan over a low heat and fry the cloves for about 30 seconds. Add the spring onions and ginger and continue frying for 3–4 minutes.
3. Mash the swede and add to the spring onion mixture. Season with salt and pepper to taste, stir well and serve at once.

VARIATION

If you need to avoid dairy products, try a well-flavoured olive oil in place of the butter.

GERMAN KOHLRABI AND CARROTS (V)

Kohlrabi is a popular vegetable in Germany, and it is starting to appear in British shops. It grows on the stem of the plant, rather like a solid Brussels sprout. The flavour is slightly reminiscent of sprouts too. Peel the vegetable as thinly as you can and grate coarsely for quick cooking.

225g kohlrabi, peeled and coarsely grated
225g carrots, peeled and coarsely grated
300ml soya milk
2 tbsp extra virgin olive oil
2 tbsp plain flour
1 tbsp chopped fresh dill
salt and freshly ground black pepper

1. Put the kohlrabi and carrots in a saucepan and cover with the soya milk. Bring to the boil, then reduce the heat, cover with a lid and simmer for 20 minutes until soft.
2. Heat the oil in a small saucepan and add the flour. Using a wooden spoon, stir over a medium heat until the mixture bubbles.
3. Using the tip of a teaspoon, add small amounts of the oil and flour mixture to the cooked vegetables, stirring all the time. Add the dill, salt and pepper and bring to the boil. Boil gently for 2–3 minutes to ensure that the flour is cooked through. Serve at once.

CAULIFLOWER PROVENCE-STYLE (V)

Redolent of the herbs of Provence, this aromatic cauliflower dish makes a change from cauliflower cheese and it is much faster to make.

2 tbsp extra virgin olive oil
2 garlic cloves, peeled and finely chopped
½ tsp fennel seeds (optional)
1 bay leaf
1 sprig of rosemary or ½ tsp dried rosemary
2 tbsp tomato purée
100ml vegetable stock
1 cauliflower, washed and cut into large florets
25g black olives, stoned
salt and freshly ground black pepper
2 tbsp chopped fresh parsley

1. Heat the oil in a large saucepan and gently fry the garlic, fennel seeds if using, bay leaf and rosemary for about 1 minute.
2. Stir in the tomato purée and then the stock. Add the cauliflower, olives, salt and pepper and bring to the boil. Cook over a medium heat for 10 minutes, turning the cauliflower in the juices from time to time.
3. When the cauliflower is just tender, stir in the parsley and serve.

VARIATION

Use 450g green beans or celery in place of the cauliflower florets; leave out the black olives, which do not work so well with these vegetables.

ITALIAN BRAISED PUMPKIN (V)

Pumpkin is often associated with America, but the Italians also use pumpkin in casseroles and in filled pasta. This recipe produces a wonderfully garlicky mixture which can be served as a side dish or used to stuff other vegetables such as blanched cabbage leaves or grilled mushroom caps.

450g peeled and seeded pumpkin (about 1kg whole pumpkin)
2 tbsp extra virgin olive oil
200ml dry white wine, or half and half wine and vegetable
  stock
2 large garlic cloves, peeled and coarsely chopped
salt and freshly ground black pepper
2–3 tbsp chopped fresh parsley

1. Dice the pumpkin fairly small to ensure that it cooks through quickly.
2. Heat the olive oil and wine in a saucepan and add the garlic. Add the pumpkin, salt and pepper and bring back to the boil. Reduce the heat and cover with a lid. Cook over a medium heat for about 20 minutes, stirring from time to time, until the pumpkin is tender. If the mixture becomes dry, add a little more stock.
3. When the pumpkin is cooked, if there is any liquid left in the pan, increase the heat to boil it off. Stir in the parsley and serve hot.

INDIAN MASHED POTATOES (V)

This simple dish is wonderfully aromatic and whatever I serve it with it always disappears very fast! I love to eat it on its own, but it goes well with any of the curried dishes in Chapter 7. The mixture also makes a very good stuffing for cabbage leaves and red peppers. Steam them at the same time as the potatoes, then fill the leaves or peppers and steam for about 5 minutes before serving.

700g potatoes, peeled and diced
2 tbsp groundnut oil
1 tsp cumin seeds
1 green or red chilli, seeded and finely chopped
1 onion, peeled and finely chopped
1 tsp curry powder
1 tbsp mango chutney, chopped
2 tbsp chopped fresh coriander
salt and freshly ground black pepper

1. Steam the potatoes for about 5–8 minutes until just tender. Take care not to overcook them.
2. While the potatoes are cooking, heat the oil in a saucepan and fry the cumin seeds for about 1 minute. Add the chilli and onion and fry for about 5 minutes until well browned. Stir in the curry powder, mango chutney, coriander, salt and pepper.
3. When the potatoes are cooked, mash them and stir in the onion mixture. Spoon into a pudding basin and cover with clingfilm. Pour boiling water into a saucepan to a depth of 2cm, add the bowl of potato mixture and simmer for 5 minutes. Serve hot.

AFRICAN RED BEANS (V)

In western and southern Africa, this bean dish would probably be eaten with ugali, a kind of thick porridge made from cornmeal. The nearest European equivalent is polenta. It is also good served with Lentil Burgers (see page 160) or Oriental Sweetcorn Fritters (see page 48).

1 tbsp extra virgin olive oil
1 large onion, peeled and chopped
1 garlic clove, peeled and chopped
1 green pepper, seeded and chopped
2 tsp coriander seeds
1 tsp caraway seeds
1 small dried red chilli
1 tbsp tomato purée
225g cooked or canned red kidney beans
200ml canned coconut milk
salt and freshly ground black pepper

Garnish
2 tbsp desiccated coconut

1. Heat the oil in a saucepan over a medium heat and fry the onion, garlic and green pepper for about 5 minutes until lightly browned.
2. Crush the coriander and caraway seeds with the chilli in a pestle and mortar or grind in an electric grinder. Stir into the vegetables and cook for another minute.
3. Add the tomato purée, beans and coconut milk and bring the mixture to the boil. Cook over a medium heat for 10–15 minutes until the sauce has thickened. Season to taste and serve hot, sprinkled with desiccated coconut.

VARIATION

If you do not like caraway, this dish is also good made with ½ teaspoon fennel seeds and 5–6 allspice berries instead.

SICILIAN POTATOES (V)

Capers are the pickled flower buds of the caper plant and they are widely used as a flavouring in southern Italy. If you find them a little strong try the milder caper fruit (caper berries), which are beginning to appear on delicatessen shelves.

Serve these wonderfully aromatic potatoes with Italian Braised Pumpkin (see page 242).

1 tbsp extra virgin olive oil
1 onion, peeled and sliced
400g can plum tomatoes
16 black olives, stoned
1 heaped tbsp capers, rinsed
1 tbsp raisins
1 tbsp pine nuts
2 tbsp chopped fresh parsley
salt and freshly ground black pepper
500g potatoes, peeled and cubed

1. Heat the oil in a saucepan over a medium heat and fry the onion for 4–5 minutes until lightly browned.
2. Chop the tomatoes roughly and add to the onion, together with the juice from the can, and all the remaining ingredients except the potatoes. Bring to the boil.
3. Add the potatoes, reduce the heat and simmer for 20 minutes, stirring from time to time. Serve hot.

POTATO AND CELERY STEW (V)

This is an easy all-in-one accompaniment to dishes such as grilled veggie burgers or tofu burgers, stuffed vegetables or nut roasts. For a supper in a hurry you can share this between two and add a good sprinkling of grated cheese.

1 tbsp extra virgin olive oil
2 small onions, peeled and finely chopped
1 garlic clove, peeled and finely chopped
4 large potatoes, peeled and diced
4 large sticks of celery, chopped
100ml vegetable stock
1 tbsp chopped fresh dill
salt and freshly ground black pepper

1. Heat the oil in a deep frying pan over a medium–low heat and fry the onions and garlic for 2–3 minutes until softened but not browned.
2. Add the potatoes and celery and fry gently for a further 2–3 minutes, stirring from time to time.
3. Add the stock, dill, salt and pepper, stir and bring to the boil. Cover with a lid and simmer for 15 minutes until the vegetables are tender. Serve at once.

VARIATIONS
Use freshly chopped sage or tarragon in place of dill.
Add a diced sweet and sour pickled cucumber for a more piquant flavour.

INDEX

THE OLIVE OIL DIET

Dr Simon Poole and Judy Ridgway

Available to buy in ebook and paperback

Recent studies have shown that a diet based around olive oil will significantly improve your health, well-being and vitality. It will also help you maintain a healthy weight and avoid heart disease, stroke and diseases such as cancer, diabetes and dementia.

All olive oils are not the same, however. This book also explores the effects of diverse varieties of olives, growing techniques and oil-production methods on the health-giving properties – and flavour – of different oils. With over 100 delicious recipes, it points the way to those extra virgin oils and food combinations that are likely to do you the most good.

This fascinating journey to the heart of the Mediterranean reveals the extraordinary health secrets of nature's original superfood.

A BANQUET ON A BUDGET

Judy Ridgway

Available to buy in ebook and paperback

Catering for any large scale celebration can be daunting. Where will you hold the event? How much food will you need? When should you start the preparation? This book passes on the secrets of the trade to ensure that the preparation goes smoothly and that the food is just as good as the professionals can offer.

It includes a checklist for the preparations with general advice on choosing food and drink, buying in ready-made items, estimating quantities, hiring staff and equipment and other practical considerations. There are five complete menus and drinks suggestions for a drinks party with canapés, a fork buffet, a finger buffet and a sit-down meal, with guests varying in number from twenty to sixty. Menus include full preparation plans and 120 mouth-watering recipes.

CAN I EAT THAT?

Jenefer Roberts

Available to buy in ebook and paperback

A nutritional guide through the dietary maze for type 2 diabetics

If you, or someone you know, has recently been diagnosed with type 2 diabetes, you have probably felt confronted with bewildering dietary restrictions and conflicting guidance. This book gives you the clear answers you need.

The book is written in a down-to-earth style and explains clearly the nutritional factors behind the disease, and behind foods that are tolerated. It is filled with advice on how to choose and cook beneficial, tasty food for those with type 2 diabetes and contains over 100 varied recipes for suitable, healthy, nutritious and – above all – delicious meals.

MEDITERRANEAN COOKING FOR DIABETICS

Robin Ellis

Available to buy in ebook and paperback

The food lover's guide to eating well with diabetes

Based on Mediterranean cuisine – one of the healthiest in the world – British actor, Robin Ellis shares his lifetime collection of healthy and simple recipes especially selected and adapted for people wishing to control or prevent type 2 diabetes. He shares the recipes that he has created, adapted and enjoyed as the basis of his Mediterranean way of eating. They are reliable, easy to follow and, above all, delicious!

Mediterranean Cooking for Diabetics is not a diet cookbook, to be followed for a while before resuming normal life. This is a book that represents a whole new way of eating and cooking that is suitable for diabetics – and for anyone who wants to eat more healthily.

SOUTHERN ITALIAN FAMILY COOKING

Carmela Sophia Sereno

Available to buy in ebook and paperback

Simple, healthy and affordable food from Italy's *cucina povera*

Healthy food on a sensible budget is important to many of us today but in Southern Italy, *la cucina povera* has been a philosophy for generations. These are delicious, filling recipes that will become family favourites in your own home, such as:

- Slow cooked meals such as ragù – a delicious tomato-based sauce with meat
- Stuffed peppers, using stale bread and herbs to fill peppers prior to baking
- Pork cotolette, pork escalopes covered in egg and seasoned breadcrumbs, flash fried

It's not just about the food; it's about the whole ethos of Italian family life. Carmela shows you how to be creative with what's available to you and gives you an incredibly healthy way to live and enjoy food with family and friends.

A LEBANESE FEAST OF VEGETABLES, PULSES, HERBS AND SPICES

Monah Hamadeh

Available to buy in ebook and paperback

With its focus on vegetables, fresh fruit, pulses, nuts, herbs and spices, the Lebanese diet is known to be one of the healthiest in the world. Natural flavours and freshness are the main attraction of the country's vegetable dishes.

Whether you are vegetarian or – like the Lebanese – often enjoy meat-free days, you'll find a feast of traditional, authentic vegetable and pulse recipes in this book. These include the famous mezze and speciality sweets, hearty peasant food from the rural mountains, traditional dishes from the Mediterranean coast, and street food including the familiar falafel wraps.

These recipes show how you can turn a few simple, economical ingredients into a tasty meal with a stunning combination of flavours.

DELICIOUS GLUTEN-FREE BAKING

Howard Middleton

Available to buy in ebook and paperback

Delicious free-from baking recipes that everyone can enjoy!

First catching the public's attention on series 4 of BBC's *The Great British Bake Off*, Howard Middleton went on to win their affection with his quirky style and love of unusual ingredients.

Championing inclusive baking, Howard shows how you can create tasty, tempting bakes that are all wheat-free and gluten-free – from simple savoury suppers and teatime treats to divinely decadent desserts.

With many recipes that are dairy-free too, Howard ensures that everyone can enjoy perfect cakes, melt-in-the-mouth biscuits and gorgeous, crusty breads. His book includes practical tips on different flours and clever ideas for presentation, and is the book for anyone who wants to make gluten-free absolutely delicious!

BEAT IBS

Hilda Glickman

Available to buy in ebook and paperback

A simple, five-step plan for restoring your digestive health

Are you suffering from Irritable Bowel Syndrome? Do you have episodes of wind, bloating, constipation and diarrhoea? If so, this probably means that your digestive system is not functioning properly and you need to find out why.

Based on proven methods applied in her own practice, Hilda Glickman discusses the symptoms of IBS, shows you how to test at home for the possible causes and looks at how you can improve your overall health through simple changes to your diet.

Your digestive system doesn't exist on its own. If it is not functioning correctly your overall health will be adversely affected. This book will show you how to heal your gut, improve your health, and prevent further problems.

THE

IMPR⟳VEMENT

ZONE

Looking for life inspiration?

The Improvement Zone has it all, from **expert advice** on how to advance your **career** and boost your **business**, to improving your **relationships**, revitalising your **health** and developing your **mind**.

Whatever your goals, head to our website now.

www.improvementzone.co.uk

INSPIRATION ON THE MOVE

INSPIRATION DIRECT TO YOUR INBOX